A
MESSAGE
IN A
MINUTE

A
MESSAGE
IN A
MINUTE

Volume 2

MORE LIGHTHEARTED
MINIDRAMAS
FOR CHURCHES

William D. Wolfe
with
Sheryl J. Anderson

Judson Press ® Valley Forge

A MESSAGE IN A MINUTE
More Lighthearted Minidramas for Churches, Volume 2
© 1998 by Judson Press, Valley Forge, PA 19482-0851

Bible quotations in this volume are from *HOLY BIBLE: New International Version,* copyright © 1973, 1978, 1984. Used by permission of Zondervan Bible Publishers.

Purchase of this book grants the owner permission to photocopy the number of additional scripts needed for performance of the minidramas. Please include the following credit line on each copy: *A Message in a Minute,* vol. 2, by William D. Wolfe with Sheryl J. Anderson copyright © 1998 by Judson Press; used by permission.

Library of Congress Cataloging-in-Publication Data

Wolfe, William D., 1954-
    A message in a minute : lighthearted minidramas for churches / by William D. Wolfe
and Sheryl J. Anderson Parrott.
        p. cm.
    ISBN 0-8170-1181-1
    1. Christian drama, American. 2. Drama in public worship. I. Anderson Parrott,
Sheryl J., 1958- . II. Title.
    PS3573.O5268M4 1992
    812'.54–dc20   92-5618

    A message in a minute : more lighthearted minidramas for churches (volume 2)
    ISBN 0-8170-1279-6

Printed in the U.S.A.

06 05 04 03 02 01 99 98

10 9 8 7 6 5 4 3 2 1

Contents

Other Dramas and Themes

Preface

Drama is a powerful medium for communicating ideas and truths. It has the ability to draw in observers, involve them in an ongoing dialogue that's happening onstage, and leave them pondering a specific scriptural truth in an entirely new way. It can move them to tears or to laughter, or to any other point between those two expressions. It is one of the most effective ways to teach a scriptural truth to our younger generations.

In a church worship setting, drama can be the message, or it can be the "set-up event" for the sermon. It can allow a scriptural truth to be seen from a different angle or perspective. It can become Scripture acted out.

The minidramas in this second volume, as in the first, have all been used in worship services. Their strength is their simplicity in terms of props, scenery, and length (about three–five minutes each). They are long enough to make the point, but short enough to be easily included in a worship service. Some are written with a cast of youth in mind, others for people of any age. Many of these minidramas could even be performed as puppet shows.

No matter who is in the cast, drama that is done well leaves a lasting impression on the audience. Drama that is done poorly leaves the congregation asking, "What was that?" or "Why was that included in worship today?"

In terms of communicating the gospel message, drama is one of the avenues that the church in general has been slow to use, even though it has tremendous potential. I hope this collection of dramas will be used to further the Kingdom and communicate its riches.

Introduction

Professional training and experience in dramatics are not prerequisites for use of the minidramas in this book. They are written for use by anyone who would like to "put some drama" in their church. Almost all of these skits have already been performed by the non-professional drama troupe of the church I pastor. They were received well and added to the worship experience or group gathering.

These minidramas are designed to require minimal stage props; at most, a table and chairs will be needed. At times the stage directions may mention more elaborate props, but tables, chairs, or other simple props can be substituted for convenience. The number of people needed ranges from one to eleven. Most require a cast of just two or three.

Here are a few tips for effectively using these minidramas in your church.

1. Planning and preparation. Make assignments about a month ahead. The amount of preparation time that is needed will vary according to the experience of your cast members. An experienced cast may need only a few days of preparation, while novices may require several weeks.

2. Adapting characters. Almost all of these skits can be adapted to fit the cast members who are available. For instance, with few or no changes, many parts can be played by either a man or a woman. As a general rule, children under ten should not be given speaking parts; if a script calls for a small child, ask an older child or young person to pretend to be younger.

3. Learning lines. If you plan to have cast members memorize their lines, remember that some people have an easy time learning their lines while others struggle. A prompter can be placed in the front row or close to the action. Many of these skits allow a person to have a book, newspaper, or table in front of him or her. Scripts can be concealed there and will be fairly unnoticeable to those watching. This is also helpful if it is not possible for the cast members to memorize their lines. Even if lines are not memorized, the performers should be familiar with their lines and comfortable in delivering them.

4. Coordination with the pastor. Find out from the pastor what upcoming sermon themes will be and coordinate the use of minidramas with these themes. The pastor also should have the final say as to where a minidrama is to be placed in the worship service.

5. Placement in the worship service. Minidramas can be a hindrance to worship if they are placed in an inappropriate spot. When deciding where to place a minidrama in a worship service, it's important to strive for smooth transitions. In some situations the minidrama might be placed at the beginning of the service, even before the first hymn is sung. Others might fit best right before the sermon. If props need to be set up and taken down, this should be a consideration in the placement of the minidrama.

6. **Choosing performance space.** These minidramas can be performed in the main aisle, in the front or on the platform, or even while moving around the sanctuary. In deciding on the best place, it is important to consider sight lines, traffic patterns (of cast members, the congregation, and other worship service participants), and acoustics. Depending on the layout of your place of worship, the need for certain props may determine where the skit is performed.

7. **Using minidramas in other settings.** Some of these minidramas can easily be incorporated into other church functions. Church business meetings can be livened up a bit. Congregational dinners can have a little extra sparkle with two or three skits added. Youth meetings, retreats, and even Sunday church school classes can benefit from an occasional minidrama or two. Be creative and be bold.

8. **Writing for your situation.** You may want to use drama to address themes and issues that are not covered in this book. Someone in your church may want to write minidramas. You may want to try writing one yourself. Beginning writers will need a few guidelines: It is best to begin with only a few characters; each minidrama should try to make one point, not many; each minidrama should have a beginning, a middle, and an end; simple, spoken language is most effective (it can help to read aloud as you write); and simple props and stage directions work best. Don't let a lack of experience keep you from trying, and don't be frustrated if your first efforts aren't Academy Award caliber. With some practice and persistence, you may very well be surprised by the end results.

Remember that minidramas can help bring the truths of the Bible alive. If you can do this, you will have accomplished great things.

Class Project (Christmas Theme)

Setting: Five students — GAIL, CRAIG, BETH, JERRY, and FELICIA — are seated in a semi-circle, chatting. Their teacher, Ms. PRESSMAN, enters.

Ms. PRESSMAN: Good morning, everyone. The first thing I would like to discuss this morning is our class Christmas project.

CRAIG: Another project? I'm still exhausted from my science project.

GAIL: How tired can you be? All you did was put a couple of fleas in a box.

CRAIG: So I could demonstrate how high fleas can jump.

JERRY: Turns out they can jump as high as the principal's toupee.

CRAIG: So I should get extra credit for demonstrating how high a principal can jump.

BETH: I hope whatever we're doing for Christmas doesn't have anything to do with bugs.

Ms. PRESSMAN: I was thinking more along the lines of a service project, yes.

FELICIA: Why don't we just do the same thing we did last year? Remember, we brought all our old toys and games in and gave them to some kids who didn't have any.

CRAIG: I could go for that. I got rid of a lot of junk last year and made room for my new Super-Duper Improved Deluxe Nintendo game system with CD-ROM and enhancer accessories. This year what I need to make room for is one of those virtual reality deals—

Ms. PRESSMAN: Excuse me, Craig, but clearing out old stuff so you can get new stuff is hardly the true spirit of Christmas.

CRAIG: I'm giving, aren't I?

Ms. PRESSMAN: I assume you're familiar with the phrase, "It's the thought that counts." So when there is no thought, it doesn't count.

BETH: So maybe we should go caroling this year.

GAIL: I am not going to stand next to Jerry while he tries to hit the high notes in "The First Noel."

JERRY: Excuse me. I didn't realize Whitney Houston had joined our class.

Ms. PRESSMAN: Caroling would be nice, but I was thinking about something that really requires you to give.

FELICIA: But we offered to give toys and you said no. Are these trick questions?

4

Ms. Pressman: Giving away old toys is something you would do anyway. Singing is something you like to do, so you'd do it anyway. Real giving means giving of yourself. Doing something you wouldn't have done otherwise.

Jerry: Oh, so Craig could get smart for Christmas.

Craig: Faster than you could get handsome for Christmas.

Gail: Maybe you could both get quiet. For a long time.

Ms. Pressman: I was thinking about cookies.

Beth: Like baking cookies for kids in shelters or hospitals? That would be cool. My mom bakes a ton of cookies at Christmas, and I'm sure she wouldn't mind baking a few extra.

Felicia: My grandma makes this awful fruitcake, but I guess sick kids would rather have that than nothing.

Ms. Pressman: I mean you should bake the cookies.

(They all look at her in amazement for a moment.)

Felicia: Us bake?

Gail: Cook when we don't have to?

Ms. Pressman: Exactly.

Gail: If you want cookies, Ms. Pressman, I'll have to go to the grocery store. I might even splurge and go to the bakery. But I can't bake them myself. They'll be burnt and hard to chew and that wouldn't be much of a Christmas gift for anybody.

Ms. Pressman: If you all worked together, I bet you could bake something wonderful.

Jerry: I am not wearing an apron.

Beth: And you're not handling any sharp utensils.

Ms. Pressman: Think about this for a minute. What is the true message of Christmas?

Gail: Mail early.

Beth: Shop early.

Craig: Shop often.

Ms. Pressman: How about, "It is more blessed to give than to receive."

Jerry: That's what my uncle says when he gives me socks for Christmas.

Ms. Pressman: And if he gives you those socks with love, they are a wonderful gift. And if you bake cookies with love, they are a wonderful gift. Even if a few of them have burnt edges or chewy centers or even if the sprinkles fall off.

BETH: Sprinkles? We can use sprinkles? I love sprinkles.

Ms. PRESSMAN: Then use them with love.

FELICIA: Wow! Here I thought you were setting us up for these really tricky questions about all this deep meaning about Christmas and giving and sacrifice and all that stuff—but it's really so simple. It all comes down to love.

Ms. PRESSMAN: The greatest gift of all.

GAIL: No. Not having to hear Jerry sing. That's the greatest gift of all.

(They all laugh.)

Logical Beans (Luke 1:5–38)

Setting: A supermarket aisle. MIKE *studies a can of beans as* ALICE *enters with a small basket holding several items.*

ALICE: Are you ready, Mike? Come on! There's no waiting on register number two!

MIKE: Just give me a minute.

ALICE: A minute is all it will take for ten people to line up at register number two.

MIKE: It's just not logical.

ALICE: I know it's not, but it happens every time we go shopping. I see an opening, I run for it, yet somehow, six other people get there before me. Or the register tape runs out. Or some smart guy picks up the only bag of shiitake mushrooms without a price on it, and we all have to stand around and wait for a price check.

MIKE: I mean these beans. The beans are not logical.

ALICE: And the creamed corn has no sense of humor. What are you talking about, Mike?

MIKE: See the sign, Alice? The beans are on sale for nine cents a can this week.

ALICE: Wow! What an incredible deal.

MIKE: Exactly my point. An incredible, illogical deal. How can they sell a can of beans for nine cents?

ALICE: They put up a couple of signs, reprogram the little beepy thing in the cash register and — voilà. Nine cents a can.

MIKE: But where's the profit margin? Where's the mark-up? It must cost them at least twelve cents a can to make and market these beans.

ALICE: And they're willing to sell them for only nine. What nice people. Let's go.

MIKE: There must be a catch.

ALICE: There's always a catch with beans. Let's go.

MIKE: No. I'm not going anywhere until someone explains these beans to me.

ALICE: Remind me to leave you at home next time. *(calling)* Hello! Meltdown on aisle six!

(A CLERK *enters hurriedly, carrying a mop.)*

CLERK: Everybody step back, let a professional handle this.

(The CLERK *looks around and, seeing no mess, stares at* ALICE *indignantly.)*

CLERK (cont'd): Lady, there's a penalty for false alarms in this store.

ALICE: But this isn't a false alarm. He won't leave until someone explains the bean sale to him.

MIKE: I don't believe you really want me to take these beans home for only nine cents.

CLERK: Sir, I can understand your confusion. It's a pretty amazing deal. But we got this memo from the main office — the word came down that beans should be only nine cents a can.

MIKE: But why?

CLERK: Because our customers are pretty amazing people, so we think we should do pretty amazing things for them.

*(*MIKE *clutches the can of beans to his chest.)*

MIKE: I . . . I don't know what to say. Thank you.

CLERK: Oh, sir, you don't have to thank me. I'm just fulfilling the wishes of upper management. But I hope you'll enjoy the beans and eat them in good health.

(The CLERK *gives them both a little wave and exits, dragging his mop behind him.* MIKE *puts his can of beans in* ALICE'S *basket and starts off in the opposite direction. He stops when he notices* ALICE *is not following him.)*

MIKE: Alice, what are you waiting for?

ALICE: For you to start making sense. You're willing to stand here all night and argue with me about beans, but this kid shows up, flatters you, and you're ready to go.

MIKE: It wasn't flattery, Alice. It was fact. I am a terrific customer. I've been a faithful shopper here all my life. And now I've been rewarded.

ALICE: But when I told you it was a sale price, you wouldn't believe me.

MIKE: You were just guessing. The kid's talked to the main office. He's got good information. He's got connections. You know what they say.

ALICE: I certainly do.

MIKE: "It's not what you know, it's who you know."

ALICE: Oh, I thought you were referring to that other thing "they" say.

MIKE: Which is?

ALICE: You're full of beans.

*(*ALICE *storms off and* MIKE *hurries after her.)*

Bubble Gum Cards (Luke 2:1–7)

Setting: A park bench, stage left. HENRY enters and sits on the bench. He carries a large stack of baseball bubble gum packs, which he carefully places on the bench beside him. He opens the first pack, takes out the gum, and pops it in his mouth. He throws the cards on the ground without looking at them, then reaches for another pack of gum. He unwraps it, adds the gum to the wad in his mouth, and throws away the cards again. He continues this procedure as SALLY and TIM enter from stage right. They are so engrossed in their conversation they don't notice HENRY at first.

SALLY: You deserve to be unhappy.

TIM: Give me a break. My team just blew the pennant.

SALLY: What do you expect? You root for the Dodgers. A team that thinks September is Latin for "time to choke."

TIM: Yeah? Well, your Indians just got lucky.

SALLY: Luck has nothing to do with it. It's about skill. It's about determination. It's about — the most awful thing I've ever seen.

TIM: What?

SALLY: *(pointing to HENRY)* Look at what he's doing! *(calling)* Have you lost your mind?

(SALLY and TIM immediately start gathering up the baseball cards HENRY has tossed aside. HENRY glances at them with little interest.)

TIM: Are you some kind of space case? *(holding up a card)* You threw away a mint condition Jeff Bagwell. Do you know what this is worth?

HENRY: Can't be worth much. I only paid a quarter for the gum.

SALLY: But that's the incredible thing about baseball cards. You can get them for almost nothing, and they can turn out to be priceless.

HENRY: Oh, man, what are you guys, some kind of baseball fanatics?

SALLY: It's an amazing game. Have you ever watched it?

HENRY: Nah. I don't believe in organized sports.

TIM: So you don't even know who Jeff Bagwell is.

HENRY: No, and I don't want to hear about him.

TIM: But he's done some wonderful things.

HENRY: Look, if any of these guys on any of these cards were worth knowing, don't you think the cards would be a little more expensive? Or harder to get? Or at least come with a steak or caviar instead of plain old bubble gum?

SALLY: But the packaging doesn't matter. It's knowing what the cards represent that gives them value.

HENRY: Listen, I only care about the gum. And I just want to chew it in peace. If you people want to get all excited about some little pictures printed on cheap cardboard, then have a blast.

(HENRY tosses the rest of his packages to SALLY and TIM. HENRY starts away.)

SALLY: This is really generous of you, but we'd really rather share these with you than have you give them to us and walk away.

HENRY: Look. I don't care about the cards and, in all honesty, the gum's not all that great either.

TIM: Maybe you'd like the gum better if you learned to appreciate the cards.

HENRY: No, maybe I should just look for better gum. Something with flashier packaging, better freebies. That'll taste better.

SALLY: Don't count on it. Sometimes the most delicious treats come in the simplest packages.

HENRY: Stick with the baseball thing, lady. You'll never make it in business.

(HENRY exits.)

SALLY: This is so sad. He's missing out on so much. We should stop him, make him understand that he has to start collecting cards.

TIM: Sally, if he doesn't care about baseball, there's no point in his collecting cards.

SALLY: I guess you're right. But now who am I going to give this beautiful new Greg Maddux card to?

(SALLY starts offstage. TIM hurries after her.)

TIM: Who? Who's your best buddy? Who loves baseball just as much as you do? C'mon, Sally. I'll root for the Indians next year!

Sitting with Hope (Luke 24:1–8)

Setting: Chairs to suggest the back pew of a church. FRANK sits in the pew, studying a worship bulletin. HOPE enters and approaches him.

HOPE: Excuse me. Is this seat taken?

FRANK: No, ma'am. Make yourself comfortable.

HOPE: *(sitting)* Thank you, young man. You're very kind.

FRANK: It's my pleasure. Besides, if you don't sit down soon, there may not be anywhere to sit. Christmas Eve always packs them in around here.

HOPE: There's nothing quite so lovely as a full church.

FRANK: Are you in town visiting for the holidays?

HOPE: Oh, no. I'm a member of this congregation.

FRANK: Oh, I'm sorry. It's just that — well, you don't look that familiar.

HOPE: I'm here all the time. But I'm often working during the service, helping out behind the scenes as it were, so when I do sit down, I don't always sit in the same place.

FRANK: *(a small smile)* We always sit in the fourth row back, left of the center aisle.

HOPE: Why aren't you sitting there tonight?

FRANK: I started to, but it just didn't feel right. You see, my wife's in the hospital. I wasn't going to come at all tonight, but she made me promise. So I came, but for some reason, I felt more comfortable sitting here.

HOPE: *(taking his hand)* I'm so glad. Now we can sit together.

(FRANK looks at her a moment, starts to take his hand back, but decides not to.)

FRANK: I'm sorry I didn't recognize you as a member. I just figured, Christmas Eve, never seen her, she must be one of those twice-a-year Christians.

HOPE: Oh, I certainly like to stand out on Christmas and Easter, but I really am here all year 'round. In the nursery, the Sunday school rooms, the pastor's study....

FRANK: Funny we haven't run into each other, then. I'm here all the time, too. Sunday morning, Sunday evening, men's prayer breakfasts, building and grounds committee....

HOPE: And yet we've never met. Busy, involved members like you I usually meet early on.

FRANK: Well, you said you spend a lot of time in the nursery. I'm not up there much.

HOPE: I think you've just never wanted to sit with me before.

(Now FRANK takes back his hand.)

FRANK: I'm married, lady.

HOPE: I know. And I can tell how much you love her. That's why I wanted to sit with you tonight, even though you've never paid much attention to me before. Of course, a lot of members of this congregation pay no attention to me. Some Sundays, I can't find a single soul to sit with. Some days, I can barely persuade them to let me in the front door.

FRANK: This church is open to all. We take pride in that.

HOPE: You also take pride in doing things on your own, taking care of things by yourself — makes somebody like me feel pretty unnecessary.

FRANK: They always need people on the Evangelism Committee.

HOPE: I'm looking for a more personal connection. That's why I spend so much time up in the nursery. They really need me up there.

FRANK: You're good with kids?

HOPE: I'm the reason those kids are here. And tonight, I'm the reason you're here.

FRANK: Lady, I don't mean to be rude on Christmas Eve, but you are making no sense at all.

HOPE: Frank, you're a dutiful Christian. And I admire that. But there's a big part of a truly full relationship with Christ that you're missing, because you want to take care of everything yourself. But you can't take care of everything yourself. If you could, you'd be sitting with your wife tonight, not me, right?

FRANK: Excuse me. I think I'll sit somewhere else.

HOPE: Frank, no. Stay here. Look at me. You know me. We grew up together.

FRANK: What?

HOPE: I was with you when your parents brought you home from the hospital. When your Little League team won the championship, even though you were the underdogs. When you got your scholarship to college. When you asked your wife to marry you.

FRANK: Lady, I don't know you.

HOPE: Yes, you do. You just haven't seen me in a long time. But I've been waiting, because I knew you would need me again. Because I was sure I was going to be able to help you again. And that's why I'm so glad to be sitting with you tonight. Because I want to help you, and I think you're ready to let me help you.

FRANK: Who are you?

HOPE: My name is Hope.

(She holds her arms open to FRANK. They embrace.)

Moved (Luke 24:1–8)

Setting: A receptionist's desk with a sign reading "INFORMATION." The RECEPTIONIST *sits at the desk as* STEVE *and* BILL *enter.*

STEVE: Good morning.

RECEPTIONIST: Good morning. May I help you?

STEVE: Yes, we're here to see Mr. Christ.

RECEPTIONIST: Oh. Oh, dear.

BILL: Is there a problem?

RECEPTIONIST: Do you have an appointment?

STEVE: No. We were under the impression that we could stop by any time, that he had an open door policy.

BILL: He practically said as much. "Knock and the door shall be opened to you," I think was how he put it. We were there. The big rally.

RECEPTIONIST: Oh, of course. The speech on the mountain.

STEVE: Excellent message.

BILL: My favorite part was the "log in the eye." He should put that on T-shirts. He'd make millions.

RECEPTIONIST: We're not really into merchandising. Though we do offer copies of the speech.

STEVE: Trust me, I already have it memorized. What we want to do is talk to him.

RECEPTIONIST: I'm sorry, but he's not in the office.

STEVE: Has he gone to lunch?

BILL: Probably went fishing again.

RECEPTIONIST: Actually, he's moved. If you heard the whole speech on the mountain, you must have heard him explaining that he was moving to a new address, that he'd only be here in town a couple more days.

STEVE: I don't remember his saying anything like that.

BILL: Is this some sort of advertising gimmick? Make him harder to find so we'll buy extra copies of the speech or something?

RECEPTIONIST: I told you, merchandising isn't our concern. Did you gentlemen attend the big fish fry?

STEVE: The first Promise Keepers' gathering?

BILL: You bet. We were two of the five thousand.

RECEPTIONIST: Five thousand men. There were women and children there, too. And everyone got fed. That's one for the record books. Anyway, right after the meal, he made a statement. Let me check the transcript, get it right. *(reading)* He said, "The Son of Man must suffer many things and be rejected by the elders, chief priests, and teachers of the law, and he must be killed, and on the third day be raised to life."

BILL: That sounds vaguely familiar.

STEVE: But come on. That was just fancy talk. Metaphors and all that stuff. A fish story to go with the fish fry, right?

(The RECEPTIONIST shakes her head.)

BILL: You know how guys like their big stories. He was just stretching the truth a little to make the story better.

(The RECEPTIONIST shakes her head again.)

BILL: Well, that really stinks. What's the world coming to when you have to believe what a guy says to you?

RECEPTIONIST: Everything he says is the truth. No fish stories. No stretched truths. Just the facts. Reality. The ultimate reality.

STEVE: So he's really gone?

RECEPTIONIST: He's moved to a new address.

STEVE: Can we see him there?

RECEPTIONIST: Eventually.

BILL: Will he be coming back here any time soon?

RECEPTIONIST: Absolutely, but I don't know exactly when.

BILL: And we're just supposed to hang around and wait for him.

RECEPTIONIST: There's plenty you can do while you're waiting. Didn't his speeches give you any ideas at all?

STEVE: Well, yeah, but... We really wanted to see him.

RECEPTIONIST: And you will, but not today. Gentlemen! This is good news. You two act like the world is coming to an end.

BILL: Forgive us for being a little disappointed.

STEVE: Disappointed? I'm crushed.

RECEPTIONIST: Gentlemen, frankly, if he were still here — now that would be a tragedy.

(BILL and STEVE look at her, still puzzled.)

Crossword Puzzlers (Luke 24:13–35)

Setting: Two chairs at center stage. RALPH *sits in one chair, working on a crossword puzzle.*

RALPH: Thirty-three down. Seven letters. "To fray or chafe." Fourth letter is "z." Hmmmm. . . . Oh! "Frazzle." *(He writes his answer.)* Okay, so, thirty-three across. Six letters. "A painting on fresh plaster." Hey, easy. That's "fresco."

(He writes in the new answer as LINDA *enters.)*

LINDA: Ralph, aren't you ready to go yet? The mall isn't open all night, you know.

RALPH: I just want to finish this. I'm almost done, just a couple of tricky ones left. Help me out. What's the capital of Northwestern Ethiopia?

LINDA: How many letters?

RALPH: Six. Last letter is "r."

LINDA: Then I believe that would be Gondar. G-O-N-D-A-R.

RALPH: I love you when you know the answers. Try this one. Ten letters. Third letter is "p." "An instrument using the altitude-pressure dependence of boiling points to determine land elevations."

LINDA: Oh, Ralph, come on. You're just not thinking. That's hypsometer. H-Y-P-S-O-M-E-T-E-R.

RALPH: That's fantastic. Fits perfectly.

LINDA: I was just looking at my hypsometer the other day and thinking it's really time to replace it, all the wear and tear. . . .

RALPH: Sure, babe, whatever you think is best. We're into the home stretch here. How 'bout this one? Five letters. Born in Bethlehem, raised in Nazareth, crucified outside Jerusalem.

*(*DORIS *enters from outside.)*

DORIS: Ralph, Linda, are we still going to the mall?

LINDA: Hang on, Doris. We're on a roll. Repeat the clue, Ralph.

RALPH: Born in Bethlehem, raised in Nazareth, crucified outside Jerusalem.

LINDA: Begin. Menachem Begin.

RALPH: He wasn't crucified, he was shot.

DORIS: I think —

LINDA: Hang on, Doris, we'll go in just a minute.

16

RALPH: Let's figure out the words around it. Seven letters. An ascetic religion of India, found in the sixth century B.C.

LINDA: Wouldn't that be Jainism?

RALPH: Of course. I should have known that right away.

LINDA: The "sixth century" part is a dead give-away.

RALPH: J-A-I-N-

DORIS: I don't mean to butt in —

LINDA: I know it's hard to be patient, Doris, but we're almost done here. Hold your horses another couple of clues.

RALPH: Okay, the basic monetary unit of Portugal. Oh, that's simple. "Escudo."

LINDA: Is that with an "e" or an "I"?

DORIS: Oh, I bet it's with an "e."

LINDA: Doris, you always said you didn't like crossword puzzles.

DORIS: This one's making me crazy, that's for sure.

RALPH: A fruit cake eaten on festive occasions. Ends with "l."

LINDA: Simnel. S-I-M-N-E-L.

RALPH: Now we're cooking. We have "J-E-S-blank-blank."

LINDA: And I'm drawing a blank.

DORIS: *(trying to hint)* Maybe a little prayer would help.

LINDA: Don't be ridiculous, Doris. We don't pray over a silly little thing like a puzzle.

DORIS: I just think the puzzle's a little bigger than you realize.

RALPH: Okay, next letter. A small projection at the center of the outer surface of the tympanic membrane of the ear.

LINDA: Umbo. U-M-B-O.

RALPH: Almost there. We have J-E-S-U —

DORIS: What more do you need? Are you two blind? What is your problem?

LINDA: Doris, I don't think I like your tone.

DORIS: It's "Jesus." The answer is "Jesus." You can get all these obscure, meaningless facts about medicine and currency and you can't get "Jesus"?

RALPH: Wow! She's right, Linda. The next word was a mouthlike opening, such as the oral cavity of a nematode, which would be—

LINDA AND RALPH: Stoma.

RALPH: J-E-S-U-S.

Doris: How could you need to have it spelled out for you? You should have recognized it right away!

Ralph: We're not perfect. We must have been thinking about other things.

Doris: How can you let all this extraneous stuff clutter up your mind to the point that you can't see Jesus?

Linda: I guess we weren't looking for him.

Doris: Good thing he was looking for you.

The Open Core (Acts 4:32–35)

Setting: SAM sits at the kitchen table, reading. MOM enters with a gift-wrapped box.

MOM: Sam, look what I have for you.

SAM: A present? Cool. Does this mean that I'm not in trouble for crushing your marigolds with my basketball anymore?

MOM: The present's not from me, Sam. It's from your Uncle Ben.

SAM: Uncle Ben?

MOM: Well, Great-Uncle Ben Rice.

(She sets the gift down in front of him.)

SAM: So the marigolds...?

MOM: You're forgiven. Just work on your rebounding.

(SAM starts opening the present.)

SAM: I wonder why Uncle Ben sent me a present.

MOM: What does the gift tag say?

(SAM stops unwrapping long enough to check the tag.)

SAM: *(reading)* "Sam, here's an appropriate gift for you on your first birthday as a Christian."

MOM: He is such a thoughtful man.

SAM: Generous, too.

(SAM finishes unwrapping the box. He opens it to discover another box.)

MOM: How interesting. Another box.

SAM: Okay, so Uncle Ben's a little weird, too. *(opening the second box)* Or maybe, a lot weird.

(SAM pulls a third box out.)

MOM: The present must be very special, so Uncle Ben wanted to pack it carefully.

SAM: *(pulling a fourth box out)* Or he's starting a new career as a comedian.

MOM: Or he's purchased stock in a wrapping paper company.

(SAM opens the box. It is filled with popcorn.)

SAM: Popcorn?

MOM: What a great idea. You get the present and a snack at the same time.

SAM: *(digging in the popcorn)* There's nothing in this box but popcorn.

(MOM samples the popcorn.)

MOM: But it's excellent popcorn.

SAM: *(sampling)* It doesn't have salt or butter or even caramel, Mom. Some gift.

(MOM pulls a piece of paper out of the popcorn.)

MOM: Wait, Sam. There's another note.

SAM: *(taking it and reading)* "Dear Sam, there isn't anything in this box except the popcorn and this note."

MOM: I think it's delicious. May I have some more?

SAM: *(still reading)* "Yes, I have sent you an empty box. You see, Sam, the good news on your first birthday as a Christian is that the tomb was empty. Remember that. The core belief of our faith revolves around the emptiness of the open tomb. What greater gift is there? Love, Uncle Ben."

MOM: Uncle Ben is a clever man.

SAM: Smart, too. He knows we often keep looking for more when the best gift has already been given.

MOM: You're a smart fellow, too, son. You've learned a lot in a year. So how 'bout giving the popcorn a second taste?

SAM: *(sampling)* It's great!

MOM: You better believe it.

Why Can't You Be Like...?
(Numbers 13–14)

Setting: A couple of chairs at a table. FRED *paces by the table.*

FRED: Where is she? Where is she? We should have been eating dinner a half hour ago and there's no sign of her. She's probably dead in some God-forsaken alley. I thought I could trust her. I thought she was old enough to take care of herself, but obviously, I was wrong.

*(*MOM *enters from the side. She turns and waves offstage.)*

MOM: *(calling)* Thanks again.

FRED: Mom!

MOM: *(still calling)* Stay cool, dudes!

(She waves again and then crosses to FRED.*)*

FRED: Mother!

MOM: Hi, Fred. Sorry I'm a little late.

FRED: A *little* late? A *little* late? Mom, you should have been home two hours ago.

MOM: Well, someone had to stay and chop up the vegetables for tomorrow's soup and the only reason I needed to be home was to fix our dinner and I thought, he's a big boy, he'll be fine....

(She stops and looks at the empty table, then looks at FRED *and sighs.)*

MOM (cont'd): Okay, so that was a mistake. But I'm still glad I volunteered to stay.

FRED: You volunteered to stay past dark in that terrible neighborhood so you could slice carrots?

MOM: Onions and celery.

FRED: What's the difference?

MOM: I really do need to teach you to cook.

FRED: What I meant was, did you give any thought to me? I've been so worried about what might have happened to you, I've been pulling my hair out.

MOM: Don't do that, dear. You don't have that much to spare.

FRED: Why can't you be like other mothers? My friends' mothers don't run around in the worst part of town, making soup for people.

MOM: You want me to be like Mrs. Edwards and Mrs. Banks?

FRED: That would be great. Or Mrs. Thomas and Mrs. Brewster. They get together, do a little Bible study, drink tea, maybe make a quilt, then send money to our missionaries and get home at a decent hour. Why can't you do that?

MOM: What they're doing is lovely, but it's not what I feel called to do. I want to roll up my sleeves and help out right here, in my own community.

FRED: That rat-infested crime zone is not our community, Mom. If you want to work in your community, stay right here on our block. Plant new flowers in the front yard or paint the bird bath. That'll keep you busy.

MOM: I don't want to "keep busy." I want to help. And God is leading me to help in this way.

FRED: Well, you and God have your wires crossed. God should be leading a woman of your age to the Bingo table, not to the slums.

MOM: Oh, I still play Bingo, Fred. But at the soup kitchen, I can do so much — I can minister to those who are truly in need.

FRED: When you get killed down there, don't run crying to me.

MOM: If I get killed, I won't be running anywhere.

FRED: Mom! Listen to me! I want you to be safe.

MOM: If we all play it safe, nothing will ever get done.

FRED: I just wish you were a little more like the other mothers, instead of Super Senior Citizen.

MOM: And do you know what I wish for?

FRED: No, what?

MOM: I wish my son would fix his own dinner for a change.

Lemonade (1 Kings 18–19)

Setting: A lemonade stand sits center, manned by three young children. KIM is behind the stand. TRACY and JEFF are off to the right and left, scanning to see if anyone is approaching.

KIM: Is anyone coming?

TRACY: I think I see someone!

JEFF: *(turning to look)* Tracy, that's Mrs. Olson's Siamese cat.

TRACY: Wow! I guess the heat is getting to me, too.

(JEFF and TRACY return to stand with KIM.)

KIM: It's so hot. I can't believe people don't want lemonade. We should be doing a lot of business.

JEFF: And we better do it soon. We're down to one ice cube, and it's the size of a pebble.

TRACY: *(pointing)* Hey, here comes someone. Honest. A real person. A grown-up!

KIM: *(looking)* Wearing a suit!

JEFF: And a tie! He must be ready to die!

(MR. MOODY enters, looking hot and miserable.)

KIM: A glass of ice-cold lemonade, sir?

JEFF: Well, it *was* ice-cold.

(He indicates the size of the ice cube. KIM and TRACY shush him.)

MR. MOODY: Come to think of it, I am quite thirsty. I'd love some lemonade.

(KIM and JEFF hurry to prepare his glass, shoving each other around in their eagerness.)

TRACY: You know why you're thirsty? 'Cause it's hot. You know that thing that says how hot it is?

MR. MOODY: A thermometer?

TRACY: Right. The one on our back porch says it's 93, and it's in the dark!

MR. MOODY: You mean the shade.

TRACY: You can call it that, too.

(JEFF hands MR. MOODY the glass.)

JEFF: Here you are, sir.

MR. MOODY: Thank you! *(The children watch expectantly as he takes a long drink.)* Oh, boy! That sure hits the spot.

KIM: You must have been really thirsty.

MR. MOODY: More than I realized, I guess. Days like this just sap your strength. You don't want to do anything but sit in a cool basement.

TRACY: That's why we put up our stand. We figured everybody today would feel warmed-over.

MR. MOODY: You mean overheated.

TRACY: You can call it that, too.

MR. MOODY: So has business been good?

KIM: It's been lousy. Most people barely look at us when they walk by.

JEFF: Some of them say, "Oh, how cute." We're not trying to be cute. We're trying to sell lemonade.

KIM: Why do you suppose they walk right by? Don't they know a nice cold glass of lemonade will make them feel better?

MR. MOODY: The sad truth is that most people wouldn't notice a diamond if you held it right in front of their eyes. But I'm glad I noticed you. I'm glad you were here. In fact, fill me up again and I'll give you five dollars.

JEFF: Five dollars? Wow! Thanks.

(JEFF fills his glass and MR. MOODY drinks again.)

MR. MOODY: Thank you. I feel refreshed, renewed, ready to face the world again. Whenever we have a hot day, I'll think of this lemonade stand. I hope you will be here on those days, so I can return and quench my thirst. Thank you!

(Mr. Moody exits.)

TRACY: Zowee! Five whole bucks!

KIM: He really appreciated us.

JEFF: Too bad everyone else didn't appreciate us.

KIM: I guess people don't go to lemonade stands like they used to.

JEFF: They should. We could help them feel so much better.

KIM: I guess people think they can handle the heat on their own.

TRACY: You know how grown-ups are. Inrepentant.

JEFF AND KIM: You mean independent.

TRACY: You can call it that, too.

Heart for the Lord (Matthew 5:8)

Setting: A doctor's office. The DOCTOR *sits behind his desk.* MEG *sits in front of it.*

DOCTOR: I can't tell you how impressed I am by this visit, Meg. Most people don't take the time to put their affairs in order, certainly not to this extent.

MEG: People put off dealing with the consequences of their deaths because they fear death. I don't have that problem.

DOCTOR: May I say, as a doctor and as an individual, how remarkable that is.

MEG: What is there to fear when I know where I'm going? What's so scary about going home?

DOCTOR: You're an inspiration to us all. Now, let's discuss some of the particulars here.

MEG: When my time comes, I want you to use every organ from my body that you can to heal others and bring them joy and health.

DOCTOR: *(consulting a chart)* I applaud your support of organ donation, Meg, it's — oh, dear.

MEG: What is it, Doctor?

DOCTOR: Oh, I'm sorry. It must be alarming to have a doctor looking at your chart and suddenly saying, "Oh, dear."

MEG: My heart did skip a beat, yes.

DOCTOR: Well, Meg, it's your heart I want to talk to you about.

MEG: Is it bad news?

DOCTOR: Not for you, for us. As I look at your records here, I can see that we'll be able to use quite a number of your organs for transplants. But I'm afraid we won't be able to use your heart.

MEG: Why not? Is it diseased?

DOCTOR: Not at all. Quite the opposite. It's too pure.

MEG: Too pure for what?

DOCTOR: In order to transplant a heart, it must be a match for the heart that's being removed. Otherwise, the body will reject the new heart. And Meg, I haven't seen a heart this pure in...I don't know how many years. When I first started practicing medicine, I used to see them every now and then, but lately....

MEG: Surely a pure heart would help any body.

DOCTOR: Nah. Most of us are too far gone. Our bodies couldn't handle a pure heart. Send the whole system into shock.

MEG: There are ways to prepare to receive a pure heart—

DOCTOR: Now you're getting outside my field of expertise. I can only address this situation as a doctor.

MEG: Surely you must have other patients with pure hearts that will need a new one some day.

DOCTOR: Nope. That's the thing about pure hearts. They don't give out. Everything else can break down, but the heart keeps going. It's as though the heart is set on a goal and won't stop until it gets there.

MEG: Of course. And once that goal is reached, who needs a heart anymore?

DOCTOR: So you know the goal?

MEG: I do. The goal is to bring the heart back to the loving God who gave it to me in the first place.

DOCTOR: You sound like you've already met.

MEG: Oh, yes. We know each other quite well. And one day, we'll know each other even better. And you can use what's left behind, Doctor. I have faith that you'll find a way. And faith is all it takes.

(MEG *exits. The* DOCTOR *rubs his chest thoughtfully.*)

DOCTOR: Create in me a clean heart, O God... *(shaking his head)* Nah. Can't be that simple.

(*The* DOCTOR *goes back to work.*)

He Touched Me! (Matthew 5:9)

Setting: Rows of chairs representing a family car. DAD *enters and gets behind the wheel.*

DAD: Come on, let's go. We're already behind schedule!

(MOM, SUZY, STEVE, *and* STEFFY *climb in and take their seats.*)

MOM: Everybody buckle up.

DAD: Let's go!

SUZY: Mom, these socks itch my legs.

MOM: You'll live, Suzy.

SUZY: No, I won't.

DAD: Then we'll give you a nice funeral.

MOM: *(to* DAD*)* I can't believe you didn't put a tie on.

DAD: Please don't start. Why do I need a tie today? Where is it written that I have to wear a tie all the time?

MOM: I thought you liked your ties. I thought you liked the twenty-five-dollar silk tie I got you for Christmas.

DAD: I do like it. That's why I wore it last week. And got spaghetti sauce on it.

MOM: What? That's a twenty-five-dollar tie!

DAD: You mentioned that.

MOM: Why didn't you give it to me to take to the cleaners?

DAD: I left it at the office.

MOM: How could you leave it there?

DAD: I had to take it off. I couldn't walk around with a big spaghetti stain on my tie, could I? And then...I forgot about it.

MOM: How could you forget about spaghetti sauce on a twenty-five-dollar tie?

DAD: I'm beginning to think I never will.

STEFFY: He touched me!

STEVE: You're on my part of the seat.

STEFFY: Am not!

STEVE: Are too!

STEFFY: Am not!

STEVE: Are too!

MOM: Knock it off, you two. We haven't been in the car five minutes, and you're at each other. Quiet down and behave. Your father and I are trying to have a conversation. *(to DAD)* How could you ruin your tie like that?

DAD: I'm an idiot.

MOM: I'm not saying that.

DAD: Because I said it first.

SUZY: Steve is touching me and making fun of my socks.

STEVE: Am not!

SUZY: Are too!

STEVE: Am not!

SUZY: Are too!

DAD: Do I have to stop this car? This is a short ride. Can't you get along with your sisters for five minutes?

STEVE: I could get along with them better if we had a nicer car with more leg room.

MOM: Listen, Mister Man. Money does not grow on trees. Just because your father can ruin a twenty-five-dollar tie and not think twice about it does not mean that we can run out and buy a new car.

DAD: Enough about the tie. Let it rest in peace.

STEVE: Peace? What's that?

MOM: You know what peace is. Harmony. Tranquillity. When everyone gets along.

SUZY: That's why dead people are the only ones who get it.

DAD: That's not true. We can all have peace.

STEFFY: Really? Will we know it when we see it?

(MOM and DAD look at each other a moment in chagrin. MOM reaches out her hand. DAD takes it.)

MOM: See this? This is how it begins.

KIDS: Cool.

(They lean forward to study their parents and their heads collide.)

KIDS: Mooooom!

(They start shoving each other around.)

DAD: And this is how it ends.

MOM: Let's just think of it as a work in progress. Live and learn. All of us.

(MOM and DAD exchange a kiss of peace.)

Front Row Seats (Matthew 6:1–18; James 2:1–9)

Setting: Chairs suggesting a sports arena. IRENE and BRAD sit in the center seats. IRENE has binoculars around her neck. FREDERICK enters and looks suspiciously at the couple.

FREDERICK: Excuse me. Are you in the right seats?

IRENE: We are in some of the best seats in the house. Join us. There are some empty seats right behind us.

BRAD: You missed the first few minutes, but it's going to be a great game. Sit down!

FREDERICK: You don't understand. I want the seats you're in.

IRENE: I can see why. They're great seats. Thick cushions, arm rests, the whole works.

BRAD: Front row!

IRENE: Center court!

BRAD: I can almost touch Dick Vitale's bald spot from here.

IRENE: We don't even need the binoculars I brought. Want to use them?

FREDERICK: Let me make myself perfectly clear. These are my seats.

IRENE: I thought the seats were first come, first served.

BRAD: My friend Smokey at work, he told me that the weeknight games were all general admission now. So we got here early and got these fabulous seats. How can they be yours?

FREDERICK: Because, my dear man, you are in the VIP section. General admission does not apply here. These tickets were dearly paid for, and I would like to sit in them now, thank you.

(BRAD and IRENE rise, apologetic.)

IRENE: We're very sorry. We thought everyone was equal here, that we were welcome to sit anywhere.

FREDERICK: That is clearly not the case.

(BRAD and IRENE start to leave. BRAD stops.)

BRAD: If you don't mind my asking, how much do VIP tickets set you back? Twenty bucks a piece?

FREDERICK: It is hardly that simple. I made a substantial contribution to the university scholarship fund, another gift to the research fund, and I donated two brand new vans to the university fleet. And I got these two seats.

BRAD: You mean you did all that for tickets, not because you wanted to help the university?

IRENE: You came on like a generous guy just to get good seats?

FREDERICK: It's more complicated than that. There are tax considerations, too.

IRENE: Come on, Brad. This guy's right, we don't belong in this section. We bought tickets because we love the game, end of story.

BRAD: Wait, Irene. I have one more question. Sir, do you always make contributions with an eye to what you're going to get out of it?

FREDERICK: *(flustered)* No.

IRENE: You just figure people will make a fuss over you and give you the seat of honor.

FREDERICK: Not necessarily.

BRAD: Come on, Irene, let's go find other seats. This guy's obviously a big fan, and we're not letting him enjoy the game.

(BRAD and IRENE start to leave again. This time, FREDERICK stops them.)

FREDERICK: Please wait. I'd like to give.... That is, will you please take these seats?

IRENE: How much do you want for them?

FREDERICK: Nothing. Nothing at all. You're right. I have been giving with only the thought of what I would get in return. I'm here for all the wrong reasons. You're here for the right reasons. Please. Take my seats.

BRAD: But where will you sit?

FREDERICK: I think I'll move up, try to take a higher view of tonight's proceedings.

IRENE: *(offering the binoculars)* Maybe these will help.

FREDERICK: Thank you.

(He takes the binoculars and exits. BRAD and IRENE sit back down.)

BRAD: Front row!

IRENE: Center court!

BRAD: Hey, Vitale! Cover up the bald spot! I'm going blind over here!

HRPL

Give Me This "A"! (Matthew 6:11)

Setting: Dad *sits in a chair, reading.* Peter, *his teenage son, enters.*

Peter: Later, Dad.

Dad: Whoa, young man. Where do you think you're going?

Peter: Over to Lee's house to mess around with his new computer.

Dad: Time out. I thought you had a history test tomorrow.

Peter: I do.

Dad: Are you telling me that you're prepared to take it, that you have already finished studying?

Peter: Got it covered.

Dad: We finished dinner ten minutes ago. You learned all the important facts about American history from 1800 to 1850 in ten minutes?

Peter: You bet.

Dad: Then who was the twelfth president of the United States?

Peter: *(thinks a moment)* Okay, that one I don't know right off the top of my head. But I do know he came after George Washington and before Abraham Lincoln.

Dad: Wow! You really have a good grasp on the early nineteenth century. All I can say is — Go get cracking on those books!

Peter: But, Dad, I prayed!

Dad: Don't change the subject. I want to talk about your history test.

Peter: But that's what I prayed about. I prayed God would give me the right answers for the test.

Dad: Get real.

Peter: It's multiple choice. All God really has to do is give me letters.

Dad: And what if God gives them to you in Hebrew?

Peter: God wouldn't do that. Would he?

Dad: God has given you a brain to discover the riches of his world — including American history. To ask him to give you the answers so you don't have to study is a cop-out. It's an insult.

Peter: But the Bible says, "Ask and it shall be given." I asked and it shall be given tomorrow during third period.

DAD: The Bible also says, "Obey your parents for this right." And the Amplified Parental Paraphrase translation reads, "Obey your parents because they're always right, so don't even think about leaving the house before your homework is done. So saith your dad. Amen!"

PETER: This isn't fair, Dad. It's not like I'm asking God to study. He already knows who the twelfth president is.

DAD: And he wants you to know, too. Don't treat God like some magical genie who's going to satisfy your every whim. He will always give you what you need, not what you think you want. And what you need is a couple hours of studying.

PETER: A couple hours? No fair! What do I care about the twelfth president anyway? If he'd done anything big, I'd already know who he was. So he's just another guy with white hair and a beard. I bet you don't know who he is either.

DAD: Zachary Taylor. No beard.

PETER: *(stunned)* Oh, wow! Okay.

(PETER turns and goes back to his room. After he is gone, DAD looks at the audience.)

DAD: You didn't think I'd ask him a question I didn't know the answer to, did you?

Forgive Me! (Matthew 6:12)

Setting: People are waiting in a long line, perhaps at a movie theater. HAR-
RIET stands at the end of the line. NICK enters and joins the line, most of
his attention devoted to a newspaper. The line moves forward, so HARRIET
moves forward. NICK, sensing movement, also moves, but he steps too far
and runs into HARRIET.

NICK: Oh, I'm sorry. Please forgive me.

HARRIET: And that just solves everything, doesn't it?

NICK: Excuse me, I didn't mean —

HARRIET: You get to run right into people, then say you're sorry, and suddenly it's not your problem anymore, right? I really hate it when
people do that. They mess up, make life miserable for everyone
around them, and then think a little "Please forgive me" will tidy
it all up.

NICK: I don't know what to say but what I already said. I'm sorry.

HARRIET: That doesn't cut it, buddy! Do you think forgiveness is yours for
the asking? What about me? What about my rights? What about my
mental anguish and suffering? Isn't it a tad presumptuous of you to
think that one "Please forgive me" will wipe the slate clean?

NICK: It was just a little bump —

HARRIET: Oh, very nice. Try to minimize the wrong now. Why can't people
stand up and take responsibility for their crimes?

NICK: Crime?

HARRIET: It's always "It wasn't that bad" or "I didn't mean to" or "I'm the
real victim here" or "The devil made me do it."

NICK: I think we're getting a little carried away here. I did ask you to
forgive me.

HARRIET: So now you're insulting my intelligence, too. I know what you're
really saying when you say "Forgive me." You're really saying, "It's
no longer my responsibility. I absolve myself from the consequences.
It's your problem now."

NICK: No, what I'm really saying is that I regret what happened. And, at
this point, that I regret being here at all.

HARRIET: And that kind of attitude is despicable. Something tragic has
occurred and you wish it had never happened.

NICK: That I'll agree with.

(HARRIET begins to gesture as she talks, her gestures growing wilder by the moment.)

HARRIET: It doesn't work that way, bud. Suppose you'd been in a car when you committed this crime of thoughtlessness. You could have killed me. You think "I'm sorry" would have done anything then? Would "forgive me" soothe my family's grief? Would they forgive you? Would I forgive you? Do you really think I should?

(She gestures wildly and hits the person in line in front of her. Immediately contrite, HARRIET pats the other person on the arm.)

HARRIET (cont'd): Oh, I am so sorry. Please forgive me.

(HARRIET clamps her hands over her mouth as she realizes what she has said. The person in front of her nods and smiles understandingly. NICK looks on with a grim smile. After a moment, HARRIET manages to look him in the eye.)

HARRIET (cont'd): So as I was saying, no harm done!

(HARRIET and NICK shake hands.)

Soil Preparation (Matthew 13:1–23)

Setting: A work table is center stage. Several pots of dirt are on the table. Perky theme music plays as JIM enters, wearing a gardening apron.

JIM: And good morning to you, friends! We're so happy that you've joined us today for another edition of "Michigan Outback," the show that takes a closer look at what Michiganders are doing out in their backyards and fields. We've got an intriguing show for you today, so let's bring out our very special guest who's going to talk to us about the important role of soil types in crop production. Let's give a big Outback welcome to Mr. Bob Reaper.

(BOB enters.)

JIM (cont'd): Welcome, Bob! Thanks for being here.

BOB: Thanks for your invitation. I watch your show every week.

JIM: And I thought my mother was our only regular viewer. So, Bob, what can you tell us about soil types?

BOB: You know, Jim, many people planted seeds back in April or May, and they're now perplexed because nothing has grown or perhaps growth has stopped.

JIM: I've had that exact problem with my watermelons, Bob.

BOB: Melons are a tough row to hoe in Michigan, Jim, and one of the main reasons is the type of soil. But I'm here today to show you a couple of basic tricks of the trade.

JIM: Fantastic, Bob. Could we call these "dirt-y" tricks?

BOB: *(looks at JIM for a moment, then)* You can. I don't think I will. *(pause)* Now, the first mistake people make, Jim, is they plant their seeds in soil that is too rocky. *(indicating a pot)* Like this.

JIM: Say, that is rocky. What happens to a seed that gets planted in something like that?

BOB: Well, Jim, it can't get its roots down past the rocks, so it never takes hold, and usually some big ol' crow flies by and snatches it up for dinner.

JIM: And that's nothing to "crow about," is it, Bob?

BOB: *(trying to ignore him)* Another common mistake is planting seeds in a weed-infested area like this. *(indicating another pot)*

JIM: Not much growing space in there.

BOB: Exactly, Jim. When the plant tries to grow, it is constricted by the weeds. There's no room to spread out and breathe, so the plant is choked and dies.

JIM: I'm feeling a little claustrophobic myself. So it's essential to weed your weedies, right, Bob?

BOB: *(with a sigh)* Oh, yes.

JIM: *(indicating pot)* So what about this soil here, Bob?

BOB: Well, Jim, this is the ideal soil to plant seeds in. It's been loosened up so the young plant can easily rise to the surface and so it can dig down deep and lay good, strong roots. This soil will support a healthy plant which will bear good fruit.

JIM: As opposed to fruitcakes, right, Bob?

BOB: I wouldn't know.

JIM: So, Bob, it seems pretty simple to tell these kinds of soil apart. Why do people plant seeds in these non-productive types?

BOB: Basic carelessness, Jim. People don't look where they're planting and don't take the time necessary to prepare the ground before they plant. Some types of soil never give a plant a chance. And that's sad, because there is a lot of good soil out there, just waiting for seeds, and no one has bothered to plant in it.

JIM: That's tragic, Bob. Wasted opportunity in our own backyards.

BOB: It doesn't have to be that way.

JIM: Folks, if you'd like to help stop this needless tragedy and learn more about proper soil preparation, call or write to us and we'll send you Bob's pamphlet that addresses the basic issues of soil preparation. So, Bob, any words of wisdom to leave us with?

BOB: Work with the soil and it will work with you. And whatever you do, stay patient and keep planting!

JIM: Okay! Thanks, Bob, for visiting us today and thanks to all of you for tuning in. Until next time, remember — some of the best things in life are right out back!

(The theme music swells.)

Afraid to Pray (Matthew 14:22–36)

Setting: Three youngsters, BEN, EMILY, AND MARY, *sit in chairs facing the audience.*

BEN: What are you two so scared about? Just do it!

EMILY: It's not that easy, Mr. Nike.

MARY: Yeah, it might come easy for you, but we're struggling here.

BEN: I keep telling you, there's nothing to be afraid of.

EMILY: I'm not sure I want to know how to swim.

MARY: Me either.

BEN: But you've both been complaining all summer about having to stay in the shallow end of the pool.

EMILY: Just us and the babies.

MARY: It stinks. They stink.

BEN: So what are you waiting for? Praying to God to make you excellent swimmers is the first step toward learning to swim.

MARY: I'm sure God has more important things to worry about. Like how deep it is at the other end of the pool.

EMILY: Yeah, I can't even touch the bottom on tiptoe.

BEN: That's because it's twelve feet deep there.

(EMILY and MARY gasp.)

BEN (cont'd): So you'd rather stay with the babies all summer?

EMILY: No. But we're scared, okay?

BEN: Pray about that, too.

MARY: Great. So God answers our prayers and we become these really great swimmers, but then one day we lie to our parents about something or throw a rock through a neighbor's window, and then go off to the pool, but God's pretty mad at us for doing something bad, so he waits until we get out in the deep water and then he makes us forget how to swim.

EMILY: And we sink to the bottom like stones and we're lying there on the bottom, but everyone thinks we're faking because they've seen us swimming just fine before, so no one helps us and we drown. Glub, glub.

BEN: Are you serious?

MARY: Absolutely.

BEN: So, you're not afraid to pray. You're afraid of the water.

EMILY: Of course we're afraid of the water, silly. We can't swim. Duhhh.

MARY: But thanks for the insight.

BEN: What I mean is, you're afraid to pray for a solution because you won't let yourself see a solution. You can't imagine a day when you'll be able to swim, so you won't pray for one.

MARY: Now who's in over his head?

BEN: You're afraid to risk a leap of faith.

EMILY: Because that leap would be off an eight-foot diving board.

BEN: And God will be with you every step of the way.

MARY: I think I'm starting to understand. We're afraid of the water the way you're afraid of the dentist. We think we'll drown. You think she'll find a cavity and it'll hurt, so you keep waiting and the cavity keeps getting bigger. In both cases, we're hurting ourselves by being afraid.

BEN: Excellent analogy, I admit it. I'll tell you what. I'll pray about my fear of the dentist if you two will pray about your fear of the water.

MARY AND EMILY: Deal.

MARY: You know something? I can't wait until we're older and aren't afraid anymore.

BEN: What do you mean? Grownups are afraid, too. Mainly, they're afraid to admit they're afraid.

EMILY: So they keep it all bottled up. They call it "being in control of their lives."

MARY: Why don't they pray about it instead?

EMILY: Maybe they aren't as smart as we think they are.

(The KIDS shrug.)

Committee on Prayerfulness
(Matthew 18:19–20)

Setting: Four people sit in a semi-circle of chairs.

DONNA: *(checking her watch)* I think it's time to get started. Thank you all for coming to the first meeting of the new Committee on Prayerfulness.

JERRY: Boy, that's a mouthful. Why don't we just call it the Prayer Committee?

PAUL: Or "PC."

CINDY: I don't know that it would be PC to call it PC. We should be more formal, more reverent.

DONNA: Besides, I believe changing the name would require a change in the constitutional by-laws, passed by a congregational vote of no less than a two-thirds majority.

JERRY: What about right here, among ourselves? Can't we just say we've got a Prayer Committee meeting tonight?

DONNA: We'll consider that under new business on the agenda. And as you can see on the agenda, we have a lot to talk about. Being in charge of the prayer life of this congregation is going to take a lot of work, but we don't mind, do we? Of course not, because we know how crucial prayer is to a strong spiritual life, and we need to be an inspiration to our fellow members. So, where do we begin? The Prayer Vigil is coming up in March.

PAUL: And the Prayer Chain is in desperate need of being updated. There are three people in the chain who are no longer living.

CINDY: Do we have new phone numbers?

PAUL: I think they're unlisted.

DONNA: There's also the Praying Hands plaque, which needs to be updated with the names of the "Prayer Warrior of the Year" for the last three years.

JERRY: That keeps falling between the cracks, doesn't it?

DONNA: I have a suggestion on that. We could sell prayer clothes and accessories. Buy them wholesale, sell them at a big mark-up, and use our profits to engrave the new names on the Prayer plaque.

CINDY: Or even buy a whole new display case for the plaque to sit in.

JERRY: I was wondering about beginning an Annual Prayer Breakfast.

DONNA: We could schedule it to coincide with the National Day of Prayer.

JERRY: Exactly. It would be a great community event. We could sell a lot of tickets, especially if we bring in a popular speaker.

CINDY: We could serve hot cakes and sausage.

PAUL: And announce the Prayer Warrior of the Year as the finale.

JERRY: These are all great ideas.

DONNA: We certainly have plenty to keep us busy. Okay, first things first. Let's open the meeting formally with prayer. Who would like to begin?

(They all shift uncomfortably.)

DONNA (cont'd): Perhaps we each should pray as we feel led.

JERRY: Who will close then?

DONNA: I guess I will. Okay, pray!

(There follows a long period of silence with nervous laughter and deep sighs.)

DONNA (cont'd): Isn't anyone going to pray?

CINDY: I'm just not being led by the Spirit tonight.

PAUL: He's not speaking to me either.

CINDY: What about you?

DONNA: Oh, no, my mind is too occupied with the business of the meeting. How about you, Jerry?

JERRY: I'm here as an idea guy, not to handle the spiritual stuff.

(Another pause.)

JERRY (cont'd): So here's my idea. The pastor is just down the hallway in his office. Let's go get him and he can pray for us.

DONNA: That's a wonderful idea.

CINDY: After all, that's what we pay him for.

PAUL: Amen!

(They hurry out.)

Going Hogwild (Mark 14:1–9)

Setting: A catering office. Gaston (pronounced gas-TONE) is behind the desk. SAM and BETTY enter. GASTON greets them effusively, speaking with a French accent.

GASTON: Welcome, welcome to Gaston's Gourmet Catering. How may I help you today? Gaston is here but to serve.

BETTY: We're having a special celebration in a couple of days and we thought it would be really nice to have it catered.

GASTON: By all means! What is the nature of this special occasion? A birthday? Anniversary? Retirement, perhaps. We have a very nice discount on our retirement parties if the retiree is over seventy-five.

SAM: Do you get many of those?

GASTON: No. That's why we can afford the nice discount.

BETTY: This is more of a special recognition kind of party.

GASTON: Ah, a "Person of the Year," no? How very nice. This person you are celebrating is very special, to be sure.

BETTY: More than special. He saved our lives.

GASTON: I can do a beautiful big cake with a fireman on it. Or a policeman, whatever is appropriate. How many guests are you expecting?

BETTY: Let's see. There's the Eleven, plus Mary and Martha, I'm sure, his mom....Let's say thirty people.

SAM: That sounds good.

GASTON: Excellent. A large gathering, but still intimate. Now, what is your price range? Moderate or extravagant?

BETTY: I was thinking of spending about $2.50 per person.

SAM: Betty! How can you say that? *(to GASTON)* I wanna go hogwild. What's your most expensive banquet spread?

GASTON: For thirty people, I would charge you two thousand dollars.

BETTY: Two thousand?!

SAM: Go for it!

BETTY: Have you lost your mind?

SAM: Betty, we're talking about a celebration for the King.

GASTON: A king. I have experience with royalty. You will not be disappointed.

BETTY: Sam, do you realize what we could do with two thousand dollars?

SAM: You bet. We could throw a party people will remember forever.

BETTY: Blow all that money on one night's celebration? When we could do good things in the community that would last for years?

SAM: Betty, he's only going to be with us a little while. While he's here, let's show him we appreciate him. Give him the best of everything. This is not the time to play cheapskate.

GASTON: No, no. Spend. Spend.

BETTY: I'm not being cheap. I'm being practical.

SAM: Oh, here we go again. Practical. Just like last summer with the Tigers.

GASTON: You are big game hunters?

SAM: No, we're baseball fans. We never get to go to the games, but we had this one chance and she wouldn't let us get box seats. "Too expensive." So we sit in the nosebleed seats behind a steel beam and three drunken frat boys.

BETTY: The important thing was we went to the game.

SAM: The rain was just an added bonus, right? Seventeen innings behind a steel beam and three guys singing "Raindrops Keep Falling on My Head." Off key. With their shirts off.

BETTY: And none of it had any effect on the final score. We still saw the Tigers win. And it doesn't matter how much money we spend on the party. We'll still be with the King.

SAM: Yes, it does matter. We have this one chance to show him how much we love him, how grateful we are to him for saving our lives. Think of all the special things he has done for us. Can't we do this one special thing for him?

BETTY: But we'll be wasting two thousand dollars.

SAM: Money spent on him is never a waste. It's a gift. A gift that still can't begin to measure up to the gift he gave us.

GASTON: He must be quite something, this king of yours.

SAM: And see, Betty? People will hear about the party and they'll want to know what it's all about, what he's all about. And we'll have a chance to tell them, to answer their questions.

BETTY: So the money will be working for us. For him.

SAM: Everything works together for him, as long as we trust him.

BETTY: Oh, I trust him. It's you I worry about. *(pause)* Okay. Let's do it.

SAM: Yes! The King is coming and we are going hogwild.

GASTON: Excellent. Now, I have one question about this very special king of yours.

SAM: Look, Betty, it's happening already. What's your question, Gaston?

GASTON: Would you perhaps consider spending three thousand dollars?

Changing Channels (Luke 6:46–49)

Setting: DAD *is glued to the TV with the remote control in his hand.* TOMMY *enters and stops short when he sees what his dad is watching.*

TOMMY: Dad!

DAD: *(startled)* Oh! Son! Hi! I didn't...hear you come in.

TOMMY: Obviously. Haven't we talked about this show?

DAD: Well, I...uh...

TOMMY: Are you supposed to be watching it?

DAD: Well, I...uh...

TOMMY: "Well, I...uh..." what? You know you're not supposed to watch this. I'm really disappointed in you.

DAD: Come on, Tommy. All the other dads are watching it.

TOMMY: And if all the other dads drove their minivans off a cliff, you would too?

DAD: How high is the cliff?

TOMMY: Don't get smart with me, Dad.

DAD: What am I supposed to do? Watch PBS all evening?

TOMMY: What's wrong with PBS?

DAD: First of all, it's pledge season. Again. And besides, these guys are so cool. Way cooler than anything on PBS. Don't you want me to be cool?

TOMMY: Not if it means your being like these guys. They are no-brainers.

DAD: Hey, I'm grown-up. I work hard. Don't I have a right to watch trash if I want to?

TOMMY: A mind is a terrible thing to waste, Dad.

DAD: I might as well sit back. Here comes the sermon.

TOMMY: They're getting to you, Dad. I can tell. I hear you when you're getting ready for work in the morning, mimicking the dumb one's laugh. "Heh heh heh..."

DAD: *(laughing)* He is so cool.

TOMMY: Dad, don't scare me like this. Come back to the real world.

DAD: The real world is depressing.

TOMMY: The only depressing thing I see is you sitting here watching these two morons on TV. When was the last time we ate dinner as a family? Went for a walk together? Read the Bible together?

DAD: These guys don't do any of that.

TOMMY: They're cartoon characters, Dad. They're not real. Let's concentrate on what's real.

DAD: What's real isn't cool.

TOMMY: What's real is what matters. Change the channel, Dad.

DAD: Why? Is there something cooler on another channel?

TOMMY: I meant change it to the "off" position. *(as DAD hesitates)* Come on, Dad. You can do it. Be strong. For us. For yourself.

(DAD turns off the TV and puts the remote down.)

TOMMY (cont'd): All right, Dad! Welcome back to the real world. Let's go take a nice long walk to celebrate. We have lots to talk about.

DAD: Can we get ice cream?

TOMMY: As long as you don't use the term "cool" the whole time we're walking.

DAD: That's... fair.

(They exit.)

B-8 (Luke 9:57–62)

Setting: A Bingo hall. MOM *sits at the center table, playing a number of cards at once.*

MOM: *(scanning)* O-81. O-81. Doggone it.

(BILLY enters, looking around the room with concern. When he spots MOM, he hurries over to her.)

BILLY: There you are.

MOM: *(angrily)* Ssssh. You're spoiling my concentration.

ANNOUNCER *(offstage)*: N-43.

MOM: N-43. *(scanning)* There it is. I got it. Fantastic.

BILLY: Mom, what are you doing?

MOM: I'm building a laser-guided missile. What does it look like I'm doing? I'm playing Bingo.

BILLY: For the fifth time this week.

ANNOUNCER: I-22.

MOM: So you're keeping track of my schedule now? You're such a thoughtful son.

BILLY: Someone needs to keep track of it for you, since you seem to have forgotten that tonight is Sara's dance recital.

ANNOUNCER: B-9.

MOM: *(scanning)* B-9…Doggone it, I need B-8. B-8.

BILLY: Mom, are you going to sit here and play Bingo and miss your daughter's dance recital?

MOM: Billy, I am in the middle of a hot game here. Everything else can wait until I'm done.

BILLY: I see. I didn't realize how important this game was. And how unimportant everything else is.

ANNOUNCER: G-87.

MOM: G-87…G-87…

BILLY: I cannot believe this. My mother, the Bingo junkie.

MOM: I am not a Bingo junkie.

BILLY: Five nights in one week. Mom, you wouldn't let me eat ice cream five nights a week.

MOM: Of course not. Bad for your teeth.

ANNOUNCER: B-7.

MOM: No, I need B-8!

BILLY: Mom, what's happening to you? You used to watch us every minute, make sure our homework was done before we went near the TV, didn't miss a single Little League game or dance recital.

MOM: Same mom, just playing a new game.

ANNOUNCER: O-83.

BILLY: And everything else takes a back seat to that? Mom, we need you. More than ever. But since Dad left, it's like you've left, too. Don't you care about how we're doing?

ANNOUNCER: N-56.

MOM: N-56? Come on, is it too much to ask to get B-8? I need it on two cards.

BILLY: Our family is falling apart and you want to play Bingo. Sara is home, crying her eyes out because you don't care about her dance recital, and you're playing Bingo.

MOM: I just want to win one little game, Billy. Be a winner once in my life. Give me a break.

ANNOUNCER: I-30.

MOM: I-30...

BILLY: I want to give you a break, Mom. I want to give us all a break. I want us to move forward, get past the sadness of Dad leaving and start fresh. But you want to play Bingo.

ANNOUNCER: B-10.

MOM: No, I need B-8! B-8!

BILLY: I hope you get it, Mom. I hope you win your game and that it makes everything all better. I'd love to stay and watch your victory, but I need to get home and drive Sara to her recital. Have fun, Mom. We're moving on.

(BILLY exits. MOM stares after him, perplexed.)

ANNOUNCER: B-8.

MOM: (excited) B-8!

(She starts to shout "Bingo," but stops. She looks down at her cards, then toward the door where BILLY just left. She thinks a moment, then tips over all her Bingo cards and hurries after BILLY.)

MOM (cont'd): (calling) Billy, don't leave without me!

Insider Soul Wash (Luke 11:39–41)

Setting: A CLERK sits behind a counter, talking on the phone.

CLERK: *(into phone)* Yesiree. We've got an opening at 3:15 this afternoon. Bring her on in and we'll give her the works. Believe me, we'll make her look like the car you drove out of the showroom.... Thank you, sir. Bye now.

(As the CLERK hangs up, DON enters with an old pot and a large bag and walks up to the counter.)

CLERK: Good morning. Welcome to New Shine Renewal Corporation. What can I help you with today?

DON: I saw your ad in the phone book and thought it might be worth a try. Your ad did say, "We'll make it look like new, no matter what it is."

CLERK: That's right. Our slogan is, "In a jiffy, we'll make it spiffy."

DON: Can you make this pot look like new?

CLERK: In a jiffy.

DON: How about old family pictures that are fading? Can you spruce them up?

CLERK: Nice and spiffy.

DON: Okay, then I'll leave these with you, too.

(He takes a photo album out of the bag and hands it to the CLERK. The CLERK hands him a form.)

CLERK: It'll take about ten days. If I can get you to fill out this information sheet, we'll be all set.

DON: This is so wonderful that you can do all this.

CLERK: The marvels of modern technology.

(DON moves aside to fill out his form as DEBBIE enters.)

CLERK: Good morning. Welcome to New Shine Renewal Corporation. What can I help you with today?

DEBBIE: I saw your ad in the phone book.

DON: *(looking up)* You, too?

CLERK: It's a wonderful ad, isn't it.

DEBBIE: I was particularly struck by that one line —

DON: "We'll make it look like new, no matter what it is."

DEBBIE: Exactly.

CLERK: Brings people in all day long. So what can we help you clean up?

DEBBIE: My soul.

CLERK: No problem at all. In fact, we can do the whole shoe. The pair, even. In a jiffy.

DEBBIE: I don't mean my shoes.

CLERK: Oh, now, if you have a fish that needs to be cleaned, well, that's not really "cleaning" and you should really go see a butcher.

DEBBIE: No, I mean my soul. S-O-U-L.

CLERK: *(stares a moment)* Like your inside-of-you soul?

DEBBIE: Yes. I've been feeling really crummy on the inside lately and I'd like my soul made shiny and new.

CLERK: Oookay. Well, now, here's the problem. We don't do souls here.

DEBBIE: But your ad said, "No matter what it is."

CLERK: Yes, well, but it is just an ad, isn't it. I mean you can't expect us to clean something we can't see, can you?

DEBBIE: You might have mentioned that in the ad. It would have saved me a long drive down here.

CLERK: I'll mention your unhappiness to the manager.

DEBBIE: But I have to take my unhappiness with me when I go.

CLERK: I really wish you would. Any time now.

DEBBIE: Isn't there anything you can do? I feel so dirty on the inside.

DON: I don't mean to eavesdrop, but would you mind telling me why?

DEBBIE: I think it's because all I've been worried about is how I look on the outside — how I dress, how I do my hair, who I hang out with, what I talk about. . . . I wanted all that to be perfect, so it's all I thought about. And then I suddenly realized that the outer me is in great shape and the inner me is dusty and grimy and neglected.

CLERK: Well, if you've been treating your car the same way, we can take care of it. Your house? We'll send a mobile team right over. But there's nothing we can do about your soul.

DEBBIE: So I'm stuck with this inner dinginess.

DON: You could try a dose of the gospel message.

DEBBIE: The gospel? Please. I went to Sunday school as a kid and memorized all the pretty words and songs, but it hasn't helped me one bit.

DON: The gospel isn't about learning verses. It's about changing inwardly.

CLERK: You trying to steal our business, sir?

Don: You said you can't help her. I think the gospel can.

Debbie: All I want is something to flush all the sludge out of my soul.

Clerk: Please don't be so graphic.

Don: The gospel isn't a can of Drano, but it will work with you if you work with it. Little by little, you will be renewed and transformed.

Debbie: What a great idea. I'll give it a try. Thank you so much.

Don: Don't thank me. Thank God.

(Debbie exits.)

Clerk: *(calling after her)* Tell your friends about us. At least, the ones we might be able to help.

(Don chuckles and shakes his head.)

Totally Awesome (Acts 2:42–47)

Setting: Two men stand at a bus stop. HERB *is dressed like a jet-setter.* FELIX *is casual and has a Bible tucked under his arm.*

HERB: *(glancing at Bible)* So. You're a church-going man.

FELIX: Yes, I am.

HERB: I thought so. I noticed the Bible under your arm.

FELIX: I'm impressed. Not everyone can recognize the Holy Bible so easily.

HERB: Oh, sure. I go to church, too. A couple of times a year.

FELIX: Easter and Christmas?

HERB: No, no. The big holidays. Mother's Day and Father's Day. I go with my mom and dad. Makes 'em all happy and weepy and they get to show me off to their friends, and then we go out and do *(indicating quotation marks)* "the fam thing." I don't really mind doing it, because it gets the 'rents so jazzed, but I cannot stay awake once the service gets going. I do my heavy partying on Saturday night, and staying awake for anything on Sunday is a real battle. And when the battle is between sleep and a boring sermon, guess who's going to win?

FELIX: Have you ever tried an Easter service?

HERB: Oh, sure. Been to a couple, in fact. But that lazy pastor tells the same story every year. Been there, heard that. I'd rather sleep.

FELIX: I'm very sorry.

HERB: What's to be sorry about? I'm not missing anything. And I'm getting the sleep I need to stay a healthy party animal. C'mon, admit it. You catch a few winks during your pastor's sermon, don't you?

FELIX: No.

HERB: Man, what church do you belong to?

FELIX: I'm a member of the Cowabunga Dude Church of the Totally Awesome Lord.

HERB: You're making fun of me.

FELIX: Not at all. I'm very serious about the Cowabunga Dude Church of the Totally Awesome Lord.

HERB: That doesn't sound like a church. It sounds like a cult. Or maybe a tax shelter.

FELIX: No, we're a church. A church that believes our God is an awesome God. Haven't you heard the song? "Our God is an awesome God, He reigns in heaven above."

HERB: You sound excited when you talk about it.

FELIX: I'm excited whenever I think about it.

HERB: You mean to tell me, you get into church? It moves you and grooves you?

FELIX: Completely. We are awed by the moving of God's spirit among us. That's the coolest groove there is. It's fantastic.

HERB: And awesome?

FELIX: Totally. You should come check it out.

HERB: I can't. I already promised my mom I'd take her to church for Mother's Day.

FELIX: It's only January.

HERB: I like to plan ahead.

FELIX: Come this Sunday.

HERB: It's only January.

FELIX: And you can still go with your mother in May.

HERB: My poor dad is going to feel totally left out.

FELIX: You can go with him in June! You can attend every week.

HERB: That's a radical concept.

FELIX: It's a radical faith. It will change your life.

HERB: It certainly will. It'll make me sick.

FELIX: What?

HERB: You're talking about my giving up some of the best sleep I get all week. I'll have mono in no time.

FELIX: I am talking about something that will strengthen you, lift you up, and make you whole. You'll be a new man in no time.

HERB: For real?

FELIX: *(handing him the Bible)* It's all in the instruction manual. Skip the nap and give us a try.

HERB: Awesome!

Essential Vitamins (Acts 15)

Setting: A supermarket checkout line. GAIL stands in line with a bottle of vitamins. WANDA enters with a basket brimming with purchases and gets in line behind GAIL.

WANDA: Buying vitamins, huh?

GAIL: Yes.

WANDA: Just buying vitamins.

GAIL: Yes.

WANDA: Just the one bottle of vitamins.

GAIL: Yes. Is there a two-for-one sale that I missed?

WANDA: No, I'm just surprised that you're only buying one bottle of vitamins.

GAIL: I know, it seems silly to come all the way to the store for one item, but my husband just did the grocery shopping yesterday and he forgot the vitamins. So I had to come back for them. I'm just glad he didn't forget the toilet paper. I hate buying just toilet paper. People look at you funny.

WANDA: They're just wondering how fast you need to get home. What I really meant was, I'm surprised that you're just buying one kind of vitamin.

GAIL: It has everything I need. All my daily requirements.

WANDA: Like you know what your daily requirements are.

GAIL: For one thing, they're printed here on the label.

WANDA: That's a lot of government mumbo-jumbo, brought to you by the same folks who brought you the national debt.

GAIL: Well, for another thing, I feel great.

WANDA: But you could feel so much better.

GAIL: How?

WANDA: By taking more vitamins.

GAIL: I really have everything I need.

(WANDA starts showing her numerous bottles of vitamins.)

WANDA: What about High Protein Oyster Shell calcium tablets? Fish Oil, for the cholesterol. Superwoman Carbohydrate Supplements, for energy. Muscle toners, Vitamin C, anti-oxidants, herbal essences and extracts —

GAIL: You take all of those vitamins?

WANDA: That's why I'm in the incredible shape I'm in.

GAIL: "Incredible"? Well, let's not get into that. I just wonder, does your body really need all this? Aren't you just...confusing it?

WANDA: I'm priming my body to operate at maximum efficiency.

GAIL: Wouldn't it operate more efficiently if you simply gave it what it needs and let it do its work?

WANDA: No way. The more, the merrier. Besides, if one vitamin stops working, you've got another one already in your system to take its place. Covering all the options.

GAIL: *(holding up her bottle)* I have one option. And I have it covered. This works for me. I don't need all this fancy stuff. I trust what I have.

WANDA: You clearly need more magnesium for brain power because you are not making any sense.

GAIL: Thank you for your concern, but I don't need anything else. This is simple, but it's powerful and it really works.

WANDA: Okay, lady. I tried to help you. It's your funeral.

GAIL: No, it's my life.

Fishing Tackles (Acts 15)

Setting: PHIL *and* WALT, *both in fishing gear, enter.*

PHIL: ...and so the man looks at his wife and says, "Frog legs, dear! Frog legs!"

(They laugh heartily.)

WALT: Boy, I don't know where you pick up these jokes. I never hear any good jokes, except from you.

PHIL: No joking?

WALT: Right! *(laughs again, then takes a deep breath)* Boy, nothing like the early morning freshness of a lake. Isn't this great?

PHIL: Nothing better in life than fishing on a lake like this in the sweet silence of the sunrise.

WALT: Well, except for Erma's homemade apple pie, there's nothing better.

PHIL: What would we do if we couldn't fish?

WALT: Dream about it and cry a lot.

PHIL: Do you know what a guy I work with said to me the other day? He said, "I don't see what's so great about fishing."

WALT: Is this another joke?

PHIL: No. I couldn't believe it either.

WALT: Obviously, the poor man has never fished.

PHIL: Yes, he's one of those "golfers."

WALT: Well, that explains it. Golf is the most ridiculous game ever created. Imagine, grown men chasing a little white ball around a few acres of grass and trying to get it into a little hole in the ground.

PHIL: And they try to tell us it's relaxing.

WALT: My neighbor threw his golf clubs in a pond a couple of weeks ago. Swore he'd never play again. Last week, he went out and bought another set.

PHIL: They're all crazy.

WALT: Makes me that much prouder to be a fisherman.

PHIL: I just wish I'd found out you fished a long time ago. We could have been fishing buddies for years.

WALT: Well, I always used to fish with this one buddy of mine, but he got transferred out of state.

PHIL: And I always fished with my dad, and he fished with his dad.... It was a family tradition. And it's one of the things I miss most now that Dad's gone.

WALT: What say we start a new tradition? Best buddies fishing together. May this be the first of many wonderful trips.

PHIL: Amen!

WALT: So let's hang some bait and get to it.

PHIL: You got it. I brought a whole mess of night crawlers that are just aching to take a dip. Help yourself.

WALT: Night crawlers? You use night crawlers?

PHIL: My family has used night crawlers since time began. God put night crawlers on this earth just for fishermen. What else is there for bait?

WALT: Super Improved Glo-Widgets!

PHIL: Glo-what?

WALT: Super Improved Glo-Widgets. It's the latest in fishing technology. They attract fish like flies to honey. Haven't you read the studies?

PHIL: No. Never even heard of Glo-whatsies.

WALT: And you consider yourself a fisherman?

PHIL: Yes, I do. Which is why I use nothing but night crawlers. It's nature's way.

WALT: Fishing isn't about nature, it's about catching fish. And these babies haul them in by the bucketful. And they come in seven different flavors.

PHIL: This is un-American.

WALT: Hey, I'm not breaking any rules. I'm just using the most modern equipment available. Unlike some cavemen around here.

PHIL: I like my fishing pure and simple.

WALT: I like my fishing fast and effective.

PHIL AND WALT: And you call yourself a fisherman?!

(They turn their backs on each other, fuming. After a moment, WALT turns back to PHIL.)

WALT: Wait a minute. What are we fighting about? You fish your way and I'll fish mine.

PHIL: But we came to fish together.

WALT: And we can. Your night crawlers aren't going to scare away my Glo-Widgets and vice versa. There's no right way or wrong way to do this, as long as we remember that we're here because we love to fish.

PHIL: And because we think golf is a really stupid game.

WALT: Amen!

Bermuda Blizzards (1 Corinthians 10:23)

Setting: SCOTT *stands center stage, wearing a bulky sweater.* JAMES *enters stage right, wearing a sweatshirt and muffler.*

JAMES: Turn the heat up! Man, is it cold!

SCOTT: The paper says the wind chill could hit fifty below tonight.

JAMES: My toes hurt just thinking about it. I cannot remember the last time we had a blizzard this bad.

SCOTT: I do. 1977. It was so cold the cows were producing ice milk.

JAMES: That's cold.

SCOTT: Of course, once it gets down to fifty below, what difference does a few degrees make? You've lost all feeling anyway.

(NICK *enters stage left, wearing Bermuda shorts and a Hawaiian shirt.*)

SCOTT: Nick, what are you doing?

NICK: I'm taking my evening walk. Good for the heart and all that.

SCOTT: I meant, what are you doing in those clothes?

NICK: Looking very stylish, if I may say so myself.

JAMES: In case you hadn't noticed, we're having a blizzard. Are you insane?

NICK: Back off, James. I can wear what I want.

SCOTT: Bermudas in a blizzard? You already have frostbite of the brain, but imagine where else you're going to get it.

NICK: Hey, who died and made you my mom? I'm free to wear whatever I wish.

SCOTT: And free to freeze to death. You'll turn into an icicle.

JAMES: A really bright, kind of tacky icicle.

SCOTT: You can't wear Bermudas when it's fifty below.

NICK: Didn't the pastor say in his sermon on Sunday that Christ has set us free? That he took our sins upon himself and freed us from the bondage of the law?

JAMES: Yes. But I don't remember hearing anything about Bermuda shorts in the sermon.

NICK: If I am completely free in Christ, then why can't I wear Bermuda shorts in the dead of winter?

SCOTT: Because *you'll be* the dead of winter.

JAMES: And there is a limit to freedom.

NICK: Wait a minute. Christ's love is limitless. We gain freedom through His love. The freedom should be limitless, too.

JAMES: There's this little concept called responsibility. I can drive down the street, going the speed limit, but if there is a slower car in front of me, I don't have the freedom to plow into it.

NICK: There's a big difference between my wearing these shorts and causing a traffic accident.

SCOTT: Though if you wear those outside today, you will probably cause a few traffic accidents.

NICK: Thank you, Fashion Expert.

JAMES: Don't you see, Nick? We are free in Christ, but we can't let that freedom become an excuse for our being foolish. God has set us free, but He also gave us intelligence so we could make rational decisions. He doesn't want us to do anything to jeopardize our safety or the safety of others. Just because God gave us legs and freedom doesn't mean we should jump in front of a moving train.

SCOTT: Understanding the difference between freedom and irresponsibility, that's the key.

NICK: You're right. I'm abusing my freedom by not taking care of myself. It's cold and I should dress accordingly.

JAMES: Now you've got the picture.

NICK: I'll go put on that gorilla suit I wore for Halloween. That'll keep me warm.

(NICK exits. JAMES and SCOTT exchange a look and hurry after him.)

SCOTT: Now I've got to get a picture.

Even the Little Parts Are Important (1 Corinthians 12)

Setting: BRUCE *is center, working on a bicycle and looking perplexed.* KATHY *enters.*

KATHY: Hey, Bruce.

BRUCE: Hey, Kathy.

KATHY: What's up?

BRUCE: I'm trying to put Lizzie's new bike together and something's wrong with it. Stupid, defective merchandise!

KATHY: What's the problem? Can't get the chain on?

BRUCE: No, it's the steering. It will only turn to the right.

KATHY: Wow! That must be frustrating.

BRUCE: I should have paid the extra ten dollars and had the store put it together. But no. I had to save money and show what a great dad I am, so I lug this thing all the way home, spend the entire afternoon putting it together, and now I have to break it back down and lug it back to the store and start all over again.

KATHY: Makes me tired just thinking about it. I suppose you've already double-checked the directions, made sure you did everything right.

BRUCE: Of course I did. Not that it was easy. The print is microscopic because they cram the directions in four different languages on one piece of paper. But I checked.

KATHY: Okay, I just thought I'd ask because I know how complicated those directions can be.

BRUCE: It's the bike, I tell you. No one cares about making a good product any more. Or in customer service. Like going to the drive-thru window at a fast-food place. When's the last time they got your order right?

KATHY: I hear you. I deliberately order a large root beer now, because I know I'll end up with a small orange that way.

BRUCE: Consumer rip-offs. They're everywhere. And then business complains that no one's buying anything. Boo-hoo.

KATHY: *(noticing something on the ground)* Hey!

BRUCE: Don't tell me you want to defend big business.

*(*KATHY *picks something up.)*

KATHY: No, I just saw this. It looks like a three-quarter inch bolt.

BRUCE: Then it probably is.

KATHY: Maybe this belongs on Lizzie's bike and that's why it won't turn left.

BRUCE: Get serious. A little thing like that would not cause such a big problem.

KATHY: It could be a little thing in an important place. Check your directions.

BRUCE: You ought to run for Congress. Big national debt and what do they do about it? Lay off cafeteria workers in the Capitol. And give themselves a raise. That'll solve the problem.

KATHY: Let me see the directions.

(BRUCE *hands them over begrudgingly.* KATHY *studies them a moment.*)

KATHY (cont'd): Here it is! "Steering mechanism.... Insert number 19 into number 23 until a click is heard. Rest 23 against panel 6 while adjusting 19. Make sure hole at top of 19 is facing up. Insert 33 into hole and tighten with — three-quarter inch bolt!"

BRUCE: You're making that up.

KATHY: It gets better. "Important: Forgetting to tighten with bolt will result in steering mechanism turning only to right."

BRUCE: *(grabbing directions)* Let me see that.

KATHY: See? Even the little parts are important.

BRUCE: How can one tiny piece make such a big difference?

KATHY: When you think about it, the whole bike is lots of tiny pieces, all doing their jobs, all working together.

BRUCE: Guess they need this little fellow to do his job, too.

KATHY: Unless you want Lizzie going in circles all day long.

BRUCE: No, I've been doing enough of that for both of us.

(KATHY *pats him on the back.*)

T.T. (1 Corinthians 13:11)

Setting: The Church Council is gathered around a conference table.

HOWARD: Okay. The next item on our agenda comes from Bill.

BILL: *(standing)* Thanks, Howard. As you all know, I haven't been a Christian very long — just a couple of years. And maybe I'm not very knowledgeable yet about the Word of God, although I am learning. Anyway, I've been reading in Matthew this past month, and at the end there are some verses that tell us to go into all the world to preach and teach the gospel, and to baptize people.

LORRAINE: Yes. It's called the Great Commission.

BILL: Very nice. But it occurred to me that we don't do any of those things.

IRENE: Oh, we used to, Bill.

BILL: Why did we stop?

DAVE: It just got to be too much work. Besides, we had other things to worry about.

BILL: But haven't we been instructed by the Word of God to do this work? I feel God wants us to be doing something significant, right here in our own community.

LORRAINE: You're right, Bill!

HOWARD: Any proposals for how we'd go about that, Bill?

BILL: Not yet. I think we need to commit it to prayer.

DAVE: While you're picking God's brain for ideas, be sure to tell him that it can't cost too much money.

IRENE: Now, Dave, we need to be flexible.

DAVE: *(taking out a dollar bill)* See this, Irene? How flexible is it? Sure, you can wrinkle it, fold it, fan your face with it, and wave it like a flag, but it's never going to be any bigger than it is right now.

BILL: But God provides!

HOWARD: We appreciate your enthusiasm, Bill. Perhaps a month of prayer and meditation will make God's plan clear to us by our next meeting.

(Everyone nods. BILL sits down.)

HOWARD: Now Dave has something to share with us.

DAVE: Yes, I've been researching floor buffers, and I found a place that has the T.T. 400 on sale for a limited time. If we buy it this week, we can get it for under ten thousand dollars. As chairman of the Building and Grounds Committee, I recommend that we do just that.

IRENE: Ten thousand dollars?

DAVE: Isn't that a great price?

LORRAINE: Dave, don't we have a floor buffer already?

DAVE: But this machine is twice as big. It's so powerful, the custodian will be able to do all the floors in no time.

BILL: Ten thousand dollars is an awful lot of money, Dave.

DAVE: *Under* ten thousand dollars. And it would be money well spent.

LORRAINE: If we have that kind of money to spend, I'd rather spend it on outreach.

DAVE: We can't very well invite people to come to a church with dirty floors.

BILL: I think Lorraine was taking about "going out into all the world."

DAVE: There's time for that later. The machine is on sale now!

HOWARD: Dave, I don't sense Council support for your suggestion.

DAVE: I don't care! I'm right and we're getting the machine.

IRENE: Dave, please. Be reasonable.

DAVE: I don't wanna be reasonable. I wanna get a new floor buffer. And I'm going to get a new floor buffer if I have to hold my breath and turn blue to get you to say yes.

HOWARD: Dave, this is silly.

DAVE: I want my T.T. 400.

IRENE: You're having the only T.T. I want to see around here. I can't believe you're throwing a temper tantrum at a Council meeting.

DAVE: *(banging fist on table)* I want my way!

LORRAINE: Dave, grow up.

(DAVE takes a huge breath and holds it. The rest of Council looks at him in amazement.)

HOWARD: Okay. Let's all take a moment to freshen our coffee and get some of Lorraine's delicious apple pie.

(They all get up and start to leave. BILL lags behind.)

BILL: Don't you want to stay and watch him turn blue?

(The others hurry BILL *out with them. Alone,* DAVE *lets his breath out in one big gasp.)*

DAVE: I can't believe that didn't work. Now, I'm not going to get my buffer or a piece of pie. *(pause)* Maybe I should try this "being reasonable" thing. Seems to work for Bill. *(hurrying out)* Hey, guys! Save me a piece of pie!

The Message Heard (2 Corinthians 3:2–3)

Setting: The grandstand at an athletic event. MARTY is watching intently, clapping his hands.

MARTY: Good job, Danny! Good hustle! Nice try, Jacob! Keep with it!

(CHUCK enters and sits beside MARTY.)

MARTY (cont'd): Hey, Chuck.

CHUCK: Hey, Marty. Praise the Lord, isn't it a beautiful day? Hallelujah!

MARTY: Uh-huh.

CHUCK: No score yet?

MARTY: Nope, just started.

CHUCK: Great. By the way, nice to see you in church last Sunday. Praise the Lord.

MARTY: Oh, right. Uh, thanks.

CHUCK: Jesus is so good, I don't know how people make it without him. If I didn't have Jesus leading me each day, I don't know how I'd survive.

MARTY: Right. I'm still working on that part myself.

CHUCK: Be faithful and strong, Marty. It will come in time. You know the old hymn — "Living for Jesus a life that is true."

MARTY: Right.

CHUCK: *(re: game)* Hey, what kind of call is that? You need glasses, Ref, or are you just stupid? Geez-o-Pete's! *(to MARTY)* So, I'm so pleased you're growing to know the Lord. I know what a difference it's made in my life.

MARTY: I can see that.

CHUCK: To just let Jesus shine right through you for all to see — *(re: game)* Idiot! Are you totally blind? My grandmother's grandmother can ref better than that! *(to MARTY)* So, I'd like to invite you to the Sunday school class I teach. It's a good group of people who can teach you a lot.

MARTY: I'm not...sure. I'll talk to my wife.

CHUCK: Our class is such a dynamic group of believers, we've even named ourselves. Guess what our name is.

MARTY: I'd rather not.

CHUCK: Christ's Lights. Catchy, isn't it? We're actually considering sweat-shirts.

MARTY: I'm trying to picture that.

CHUCK: We probably don't need them because the light of Jesus shining through us is already so evident — *(re: game)* Ref, you're a jerk! Get a life, will ya? Somebody shoot him and do us all a favor! *(to MARTY)* Where was I? Oh, right. Class. It's all about letting people see Christ living in us and through us. I think you'd get a lot out of it.

MARTY: More than you think.

CHUCK: Let your light so shine and all that. *(re: game)* Give me a break, Ref. Would you leave for a buck? I'll pay you myself.

(CHUCK stands and takes out his wallet. MARTY stands and moves away from CHUCK.)

CHUCK (cont'd): Marty, are you leaving already?

MARTY: The light's just a little too bright for me. I think I'd rather sit in a cool, dark place for a while.

(MARTY walks away.)

CHUCK: Some guys can handle the light, some guys can't. *(re: game)* Hey, Ref! Five bucks is my final offer!

Re-Can'ts (2 Corinthians 9:8–10)

Setting: Three people sit side by side in chairs center stage. They are dressed identically, devoid of personality. Each has a small pile of folded pieces of paper in his/her lap.

ONE: It can't be done.

TWO: Our budget can't handle it.

THREE: Can't people see that?

ONE: We can't be expected to do anything they drop in the suggestion box. I can't believe we ever put that box up anyway.

TWO: Why can't people be realistic? Why can't they be reasonable?

THREE: Can't we take the suggestion box down?

ONE: Can't risk it.

TWO: Can't we try?

ONE: Can't rile them up.

TWO: Can't we tell them we can't use their crazy ideas?

THREE: People are cantankerous. You can't tell them anything.

ONE: We can't spend all day talking about what we can't do. We need to talk about what we —

(TWO and THREE cringe and gasp.)

ONE (cont'd): …what we can't not do.

THREE: You almost said the "c" word.

ONE: I can't believe you thought I would say that here. In church. Moving on, can't we try a cant-ata this Easter?

THREE: Have you talked to the cantor?

ONE: Can't reach him.

TWO: He works in Canton now.

THREE: Can't believe he commutes to Canton.

TWO: Can't believe a lot of things people do.

ONE: Can't things be the way they used to be?

THREE: You should see the price of cantaloupes these days. Can't believe it.

TWO: I can't bring myself to pay that much.

ONE: Guess things can't be the way they used to be.

TWO: Can't be helped.

THREE: Can't turn back time.

ONE: One more suggestion from the suggestion box. Can't we start a group for seniors?

THREE: Can't we ignore that suggestion?

TWO: We can't try new things.

THREE: After all, can't everyone see that seniors are —

ALL: Cantankerous.

ONE: Okay. Can't see anything that can't wait 'til next time.

THREE: Great. Can't we go home now?

TWO: Can't see why not.

ONE: Can't believe other churches can't run as smoothly as ours does.

TWO: Can't all be perfect.

Baldism (Galatians 3:28)

Setting: A park bench. Tim *sits on the bench, reading a newspaper.* Jeffrey *enters, wearing a hat.*

Jeffrey: Good morning. Mind if I share the bench with you?

Tim: Not at all. Have a seat.

Jeffrey: Thanks.

*(*Tim *returns to reading his paper as* Jeffrey *sits down, gives a relaxing sigh, and takes his hat off, revealing a nearly bald head.* Tim *notices this out of the corner of his eye and flinches.* Jeffrey *notices his reaction.)*

Jeffrey (cont'd): Is something wrong? Do I have something on my head?

Tim: Hardly. I mean, I can't help but notice that you really come up short in the hair department.

Jeffrey: God creates each of us as a unique individual.

Tim: How long have you been...like that?

Jeffrey: It's been a few years now, I guess. Why?

Tim: My friend Denny says baldness is the result of ongoing sin in a person's life. That God sort of, like, scalps you for being evil.

Jeffrey: What a quaint theory. Let me assure you that I haven't killed anyone or robbed a bank or swindled a business partner.

Tim: Then what evil did you do?

Jeffrey: *(after a thoughtful pause)* Probably the same evil things you and your friend Denny do.

*(*Tim *runs his hand through his hair nervously.)*

Tim: May I ask you a question?

Jeffrey: Is it about the evil I have done?

Tim: No.

Jeffrey: Then ask away.

Tim: Since you people don't sweat, how does your body cool itself?

Jeffrey: What makes you think I don't sweat?

Tim: My friend Denny says bald people don't sweat. That's why they look like giant roll-on deodorant sticks. Something about the pores closing up because the hair isn't there to hold them open.

Jeffrey: Amazing. You're being insulting and stupid at the same time.

TIM: Geez, okay. I haven't been around baldies before. I didn't know you were sensitive types on top of it all.

JEFFREY: And now I'm a baldie. I'll bet your friend Denny has taught you all kinds of cheap nicknames to call people like me. "Cueball"? "Conehead"? "Light bulb"?

TIM: Oh, man, Denny warned me about this. He said baldies — I mean, people without hair — are short-tempered and prone to violence.

(JEFFREY moves closer to TIM. TIM backs away.)

JEFFREY: Do you really think I'd hurt you?

TIM: I don't know. I just don't want to catch it.

JEFFREY: You think baldness is contagious?

TIM: Denny said —

JEFFREY: Denny said a lot, I have no doubt. The question is, has Denny ever said anything that was true?

TIM: Hard to say...

JEFFREY: Did you and Denny ever consider that God made some people naturally beautiful, and with the rest he had to add hair?

TIM: Hard to say...

JEFFREY: I doubt it's hard to say, because you've said plenty without thinking. Thinking is what's hard, but I suggest you give it a try. Baldism is just one more way that people who are afraid to think try to put down people they haven't thought about. If you think about it, we're all the same where it matters, because we were all created by the same loving Lord.

TIM: Wow! That's a lot to think about.

JEFFREY: Then get started thinking about it. Soon. Because you know what the leading cause of baldness is? Not thinking.

(JEFFREY exits. TIM watches him go, running his hand through his hair nervously.)

Hymn Sing (Galatians 5:1–12)

Setting: Chairs to suggest a church pew. Helen *and* Dottie *are seated in the pew, reading their service bulletins.*

Helen: *(sarcastically)* Oh, great! We're singing all the golden oldies today.

Dottie: Sounds good to me. It's about time we had a whole Sunday of great music.

Helen: *(re: bulletin)* And where do you see great music?

Dottie: Oh, that's right. You like those "praise tunes," don't you?

Helen: You bet I do. They flow, they move, they're spiritually uplifting. And the lyrics are modern and relevant.

Dottie: Like that one we sang last week? What were those modern, relevant words? Oh, yes. "Alleluia, alleluia, alleluia, alleluia —" Catchy lyrics.

Helen: Can you honestly tell me you'd rather sing "Would He devote that sacred head for such a worm as I"?

Dottie: Hey, that's been updated. Now it's "for sinners such as I."

Helen: And it's not in the Top Forty yet. What a scandal.

Dottie: Just a minute. The great hymns create a more worshipful atmosphere. You have to agree with that at least.

Helen: Au contraire. I can worship much better after singing "Thy Word" or "Unto Thee, O Lord" than I can after singing "Onward, Christian Soldiers."

Dottie: I happen to feel the same way about "Great Is Thy Faithfulness" as opposed to "Awesome God."

Helen: You don't feel immediately drawn into the presence of the Lord by singing "Awesome God"? But "Awesome God" is the...most awesome!

Dottie: In your opinion.

Helen: And I would much rather sing to guitars strumming than struggle along with the organ. I mean, as one friend of mine said, "Can't they take the parking brake off that organ?"

Dottie: Well, too bad. Guitars make me feel like I'm on MTV.

Helen: And that's a bad thing?

Dottie: This is a church, after all. A place for worship! *(catching herself)* Not for fighting.

HELEN: So how do we worship together when we want such a different worship experience?

DOTTIE: Do you suppose there's a way to meet in the middle? Mix our styles?

HELEN: I guess it would help if I would recognize the rich tradition of hymns and not ignore them just because the modern music speaks to me more directly.

DOTTIE: And I guess I can grant you that the church must evolve and grow as its members do and add new music, as long as it doesn't completely discard the old.

HELEN: Is this possible? Can we worship this way?

DOTTIE: I think we stand a chance, as long as we start off on the right foot and remember why we're here.

HELEN: I'm right with you.

(HELEN and DOTTIE stand, linking arms, and look upward.)

HELEN and DOTTIE: Praise be to you, O Lord!

Gray Hair (Philippians 3:12–4:1)

Setting: JEN *sits in front of her dressing table, fixing her makeup and hair in the mirror. After a few moments, she gasps in horror.*

JEN: Ahhh! Bill! Bill! Bill!

(BILL *hurries in from the other room.*)

BILL: What? Jen, what happened?

JEN: *(pointing to mirror)* Oh, my Lord! It can't be.

BILL: Yes, it is, Jen. They call it a mirror. Nifty little invention, isn't it?

JEN: You don't understand.

BILL: I'm a man. When I see a woman upset because she's looking into a mirror, it's dangerous for me to understand.

JEN: Don't you see what I see?

BILL: Let me tell you what I see. I see my wife, who I love very, very much, no matter what new wrinkle or freckle she may have found.

JEN: Oh, no! You see wrinkles?

BILL: Never mind, never mind. What do you see, Jen?

JEN: I see gray hair!

BILL: Oh. Why, yes, there it is. Lovely gray hair. One lovely gray hair.

JEN: What am I going to do?

BILL: You don't need to do anything. It's only a gray hair.

JEN: Only? Only a gray hair? There is no such thing as "only" a gray hair. This is a warning sign. A tremor before the earthquake. A shudder before the avalanche. A drop of rain before the hurricane —

BILL: I think you've covered all the natural disasters, honey. And I don't think this qualifies.

JEN: Fine. Spoken by a man whose grandfather still isn't gray. You'll go to your grave without a gray hair. People will start looking at you and thinking, "I never realized he was so much younger than she is." Eventually, they'll mistake you for my son!

BILL: Jen, stop. Change is part of life. You just need to face it with grace.

JEN: But I'm too young to have gray hair.

BILL: There are worse things, you know.

JEN: Easy for you to say. I'll bet this is stress-related. You know how hectic things at work have been. I knew as soon as I got promoted, things would go crazy.

BILL: But don't you love your new job? It's only your hair, Jen. If you were turning gray on the inside, if you were depressed or spiritually fatigued, then I'd share your concern. But this is just part of growing old together. We're both changing. I'm slowing down a bit, thickening a little around the middle —

JEN: And you leave a lot of hair in the shower drain these days.

BILL: Does that make you feel better? You'll be gray, but I'll be bald. But we'll be together. And God will be with us. The important things in life won't change.

JEN: You're right, you're right. But why is it that the important stuff is invisible and the unimportant stuff stares back at me every time I look in the mirror?

BILL: Want me to run down to the store for some L'Oreal?

JEN: No, I'll be fine. But you better snake the drain in the shower. You've lost enough hair down there to make a toupee.

BILL: Touché.

(BILL exits. JEN studies her face in the mirror again.)

JEN: First teenage pimples, then wrinkles, now this. It's just one surprise after another. What next, Lord? *(pause)* No, no, don't tell me. Just promise me you'll help me face it with grace.

(JEN smiles at herself in the mirror.)

The Gift Catalog (Philippians 4:10–19)

Setting: COREY *sits at a table center stage, studying a catalog. There are several markers of different colors on the table. He uses one to mark items in the catalog.*

COREY: Oh, and I want that! *(marks the page, continues scanning)* And that! And I've got to have that!

(DAD enters, surprised to find COREY at the table.)

DAD: Hey, Corey. Finished with your homework already?

COREY: Not quite, Dad.

DAD: Then let's get back upstairs and back to work.

COREY: I can't right now, Dad. I'm deciding what I want for Christmas. The new J. C. Penney's catalog came today.

DAD: Oh, of course, that's more important than homework. *(looking over Corey's shoulder)* What are all these marks on the page?

COREY: The blue circles are for the things I have to have or I'll die. The green x's are basic age-appropriate gift selections. The orange stars are hot new products that the analysts predict will sell out by Thanksgiving, so buy them now. The red w's stand for "wow!" Those are things that I don't really expect to get, but I'd be extremely delighted if I did get them. I mean, I would just step back and say —

DAD: Let me guess. "Wow!"

COREY: Glad I'm getting through to you here, Dad. Oh, and the pink hearts are for items any good parent would buy for his child if he really loved him.

DAD: Corey, you've marked every item on the page.

COREY: *(studying the page a moment)* Huh. How about that. Well, I guess that just speaks really highly of the quality merchandise available to the smart shopper this year.

DAD: Don't you think it's all a bit much?

COREY: Come on, Dad. 'Tis the season to be giving and making people happy, and you know how happy it makes you to give me things and make me happy.

DAD: So are you also working on a list of things you might give Mom or me as gifts?

COREY: Gee, Dad, I haven't gotten to that yet. And you should know, up front, that my financial resources are pretty limited.

DAD: And mine are endless?

COREY: That's why I'm trying to help you shop wisely.

DAD: I meant you might be looking for ways to give.

COREY: Dad, you have to remember that I'm the product — "product," I'm telling you — of a consumer society. I'm programmed to receive. And look here. Penney's understands the position of the modern parent and makes it easy for you to give. "Six months to pay!"

DAD: And six months after I give, Penney's still expects to get! Corey, you can't order a meaningful life from a catalog. A good life, lived the way God intended it to be, is about giving, not getting.

COREY: Oh, man, Dad, can you imagine my telling my friends about all the cool stuff I *gave* for Christmas? Just write "geek" across my forehead now and save us all a lot of hassle.

DAD: I'm not saying you have to be a saint, but you don't have to be Scrooge either.

COREY: But I thought parents gave and kids got. Isn't that the way it's supposed to be?

DAD: I think you'll find a few boxes under the tree with your name on them, but you need to think about putting a few boxes under there yourself.

COREY: It's just so hard to concentrate with all these toy catalogs coming in the mail.

DAD: There's clothing in there, too.

COREY: Oh, Dad. It's bad enough you're making me think about giving for Christmas. Don't threaten me with socks and underwear, too!

DAD: Tell you what. You don't get me a goofy tie, I won't get you socks.

COREY: Deal.

(They shake hands.)

Spiritually Stuffed (Colossians 2:6–12)

Setting: A restaurant table. BEN *sits at the table, wiping his mouth with a napkin. The* WAITER *enters.*

WAITER: And what else may I get for you, sir?

BEN: Nothing, I'm fine.

WAITER: Nothing? Nothing at all?

BEN: Truly. I am spiritually stuffed.

WAITER: Come now, sir. All you had was a side dish of the godly stuff. Surely you still have room for some of our other offerings.

BEN: No, really, I'm quite fulfilled. Cram-packed with Christ, if you know what I mean.

WAITER: I must say I'm stunned, sir. A little taste of bread and a little sip of wine and you say that you're stuffed.

BEN: It happens.

WAITER: Yes, sir, I will admit I see it all the time. And it never ceases to amaze me. Is it some kind of diet craze? Like that stuff Tommy LaSorda was drinking? I bet that fills you up fast.

BEN: No, this has nothing to do with weight-loss products. It's just the nature of the Spirit.

WAITER: But there must be something else I can bring you.

BEN: Not a thing, friend. I'm finally experiencing what Paul said I would experience.

WAITER: And that would be —

BEN: He said, "You have been given fullness in Christ." Boy, did he have it right. This is the first time I've felt it for myself. Before, I'd always just kind of nibble around, a little of this, a little of that, and always leave still hungry. Ordering the godly stuff never entered my mind. Until now.

WAITER: That's very nice for you, sir, but if everyone starts ordering the way you did and ignoring all our nice little sampler menus, we're going to go out of business.

BEN: Here's hoping!

(The WAITER *looks perplexed.)*

Caretaker (1 Thessalonians 2:8)

Setting: A row of chairs to suggest a waiting room. LISA sits in a chair, trying not to fidget, as the CARETAKER enters, carrying a clipboard.

CARETAKER: Hello. Welcome to the International National Urban Church of Immaculate Perfection. *(checking clipboard)* You are Lisa, I believe?

LISA: Yes, that's right. Nice to meet you.

CARETAKER: Let's not be hasty. I'm the church caretaker.

LISA: Well, you do great work. The building is so clean.

CARETAKER: That's not my job.

LISA: Oh. I thought a caretaker was the person who took care of the building and grounds.

CARETAKER: And you were wrong. Now, let's get down to business.

LISA: Business?

CARETAKER: Yes, yes, lots to do. Questions, reference checks, background information, that kind of stuff.

LISA: Why do we have to do all that?

CARETAKER: Are you or are you not interested in joining the membership of the International National Urban Church of Immaculate Perfection?

LISA: Yes, I am interested.

CARETAKER: Then we need to take care of this business. My job as caretaker is to take an account of prospective member's cares, problems, needs, etc. Then I can recommend them for membership or...

LISA: Or...?

CARETAKER: Let's not consider that sad possibility until we have to. Let's begin.

LISA: *(apprehensive)* Okay.

CARETAKER: Have you ever been convicted of a crime?

LISA: No.

CARETAKER: Ever been charged with sexual assault, drunken driving, disorderly conduct, breaking and entering, or murder?

LISA: Uh, no.

CARETAKER: I sense some hesitation in your answer, Lisa.

LISA: Probably because I was expecting questions about why I'm a Christian and how I became a Christian.

CARETAKER: *(laughs, then straight-faced again)* No. Ever been divorced?

LISA: Yes.

CARETAKER: Oh. *(frowns, makes a note)* Ever been depressed?

LISA: While I was going through the divorce, I got pretty low.

CARETAKER: So that's a "yes." *(frowns again, makes another note)* Ever had to discuss a problem with the pastor?

LISA: Ahh, yes.

CARETAKER: Oh, dear. *(big frown, lots of notes)* Do you need prayer support from the congregation from time to time?

LISA: All the time.

(The CARETAKER whistles, shakes head, makes lots of notes.)

LISA (cont'd): Am I wrong in assuming that these aren't the answers you were looking for?

CARETAKER: We are identifying a lot of trouble spots here.

LISA: Which is why I'm looking for a church. I thought church was the place to come with cares and concerns and trouble spots, knowing that you would meet people to support and encourage you.

CARETAKER: Where have you been for the last fifty years? Times change. Our church is striving to be care-free by the turn of the century. To help reach that goal, we are screening new members to ensure they won't weigh us down with a lot of petty problems. Speaking of which, ever had cancer?

LISA: No.

CARETAKER: Excellent. A point in your favor.

LISA: You don't let cancer patients join your church?

CARETAKER: That's confidential. And you'll lose points for caring about other people's business.

LISA: But that's what church members are supposed to do. What happened to compassion, mercy, and grace?

CARETAKER: Oh, you're one of those. Flinging "grace" around like it solves everything.

LISA: Doesn't it? Or can the perfect people of your congregation get along without it?

CARETAKER: *(making a note)* Sarcasm is frowned upon here.

LISA: But I thought you didn't frown here at all. I thought you wanted to be happy and carefree and only care about yourselves. That's not a church. That's a cocktail party, and I wouldn't come to yours if you sent me an engraved invitation.

(LISA storms out. The CARETAKER shrugs.)

CARETAKER: See if I care.

Waiting for Jesus (Hebrews 2:1–18)

Setting: MARY, TONY, DAVID, *and* JANET *stand in a little knot center stage.*

TONY: Oh, I can't wait to see him.

MARY: Me neither. I'm so excited, I can't stand still.

DAVID: Stand still anyway. You're making me nervous. And jumping up and down on my foot.

JANET: Do you think he'll actually come?

TONY: He promised he would.

MARY: Oooo, I've got goosebumps.

DAVID: I hope he gets here soon.

TONY: This is the most significant day of my life. More important than my first day of school, or my first home run in Little League.

JANET: When did you ever hit a home run?

TONY: My second season, playing against Tom's Sandblasting and Masonry. Put it over the right field fence on a two and one pitch.

JANET: Congratulations, I guess.

MARY: This is my biggest day, too. To actually see Jesus. Wow! Wow!

DAVID: Aren't you getting all worked up for nothing?

MARY: What do you mean, nothing? It's Jesus. Since when do you think Jesus is nothing?

DAVID: I didn't say that. All I mean is, he's going to come and then he's going to go. Over in the blink of an eye. What's to get all worked up about?

TONY: How about the fact that he's the Son of God?

JANET: Oh! I think he's coming!

MARY: My hands are sweating.

TONY: There he is!

(They gaze in silence and follow the progress of an unseen figure from stage left to stage right. They speak in hushed tones.)

JANET: He looks just like us.

DAVID: He's shorter than my dad.

JANET: He needs a haircut. And a shave.

DAVID: Where's his halo?

TONY: He doesn't have a halo, silly.

DAVID: You could pass him on the street and not know it.

MARY: He's a carpenter. What did you expect him to look like?

JANET: I don't know, but I'm a little disappointed. I thought he'd be walking about a foot off the ground.

DAVID: Or at least glide through the crowd.

JANET: He's just a regular guy.

TONY: Yeah. Isn't it great?

(They gaze off stage right as the NARRATOR speaks.)

NARRATOR: Hebrews 2:14–18 tell us, "Since the children have flesh and blood, he too shared in their humanity so that by his death he might destroy him who holds the power of death — that is, the devil — and free those who all their lives were held in slavery by their fear of death. For surely it is not angels he helps, but Abraham's descendants. For this reason he had to be made like his brothers in every way, in order that he might become a merciful and faithful high priest in service to God, and that he might make atonement for the sins of the people. Because he himself suffered when he was tempted, he is able to help those who are being tempted."

Reserved Seating (Hebrews 10:19–25)

Setting: Chairs to suggest a church pew. NED *enters and takes a seat. He is dressed a little shabbily. After a moment,* ESTHER *enters and, seeing* NED, *approaches him with annoyance.*

ESTHER: Excuse me.

NED: Good morning!

ESTHER: Yes, of course, good morning. I —

NED: It's a great morning to praise the Lord.

ESTHER: Naturally, but I —

NED: Amen! As the Scriptures say, "I was glad when they said unto me, 'Let us go into the house of the Lord!'"

ESTHER: Such a lovely sentiment. Now I —

NED: You've got a beautiful church here. A magnificent facility in which to praise the name of Jesus, our Risen Lord.

ESTHER: You are absolutely right about that. And this magnificent facility has many wonderful seats from which one can praise Jesus, and I'd like to suggest that you might be more comfortable in one of the other wonderful seats.

NED: Why? Does this one have splinters? Is there a draft?

ESTHER: No. Mr. and Mrs. Thornwood McPherson sit here.

NED: Oh, they do, do they?

ESTHER: Each and every Sunday.

NED: Well, I'm happy to scoot over and leave room for the two of them. I'd love to meet some guy named Thornwood, anyway. And let me guess. His wife's name is Gwendolyn.

ESTHER: Petula.

NED: My next guess.

ESTHER: I appreciate your...enthusiasm, but I need you to find a different seat.

NED: Really, I'll be fine. I don't mind sitting with Woody and the Petster.

ESTHER: Oh, no, no, you can't call them that. And you can't sit here. You need to move to the back.

NED: Are you saying this church has reserved seating and general admission seating?

ESTHER: You could describe it that way, yes. It's common knowledge that the influential people, the big contributors, sit up in the front and everyone else sits in the back.

NED: Let me clarify a few points. Do Thornwood and Petula have a different Savior than I do?

ESTHER: What is that supposed to mean?

NED: Is their Jesus different from my Jesus?

ESTHER: Don't be absurd. There is only one Jesus.

NED: And when we take communion, do they get a different kind of bread or a more expensive wine?

ESTHER: Of course not.

NED: And when we all die, will they go to a reserved seating area in heaven?

ESTHER: No.

NED: Then why should they sit in one now? Perhaps Petula and Woody should sit in the back today and try out a new perspective on things.

ESTHER: This is highly irregular.

NED: Listen up. Christ died and became my high priest *and* the Woodmeister's high priest. In that moment, reserved seating became a thing of the past. In fact, it guaranteed that the first would be last and the last would be first.

ESTHER: But we've always done it this way.

NED: Then you better check out Galatians 3:28: "There is neither Jew nor Greek, slave nor free, male nor female, for you are all one in Jesus Christ." A modern translation would be, "No reserved seating."

ESTHER: The McPhersons won't like this.

NED: Bring 'em down here, let 'em worship with me, and then ask 'em.

(ESTHER hurries away. NED addresses the audience.)

NED: In the book of James, we read, "Don't show favoritism. Suppose a man comes into your meeting wearing a gold ring and fine clothes, and a poor man in shabby clothes also comes in. If you show special attention to the man wearing fine clothes and say, 'Here is a good seat for you,' but say to the poor man, 'You stand there,' or 'Sit on the floor by my feet,' have you not discriminated among yourselves and become judges with evil thoughts?" Christ has given us all a ticket to the great feast — and it's stamped "Free admission." Let's go sit together!

The Shot (Hebrews 12:4–8)

Setting: A doctor's waiting room. DAD enters, dragging his highly reluctant young daughter, VICKI, behind him.

VICKI: No, no! I don't want to go! I don't want to go!

DAD: I'm sorry, Vicki, I know you're not happy about this, but it still has to happen.

VICKI: But I don't want a shot. I don't want a great big, ugly needle jabbed into my arm.

DAD: It'll be okay.

VICKI: If you're so sure, then you get it.

DAD: Vicki, first of all, I didn't step on the rusty nail. Secondly, you're just making this harder on yourself by getting all worked up.

VICKI: But shots hurt, Dad!

DAD: I know they hurt, sweetheart. I've gotten plenty of them over the years. But if you don't have this one shot now, you could get sick — really sick — and need lots of shots or worse.

VICKI: There's worse?

DAD: Much worse.

VICKI: Can't I just take lots of vitamins? Eat all my vegetables every night for the rest of my life?

DAD: That's not the way it works.

VICKI: You know, if doctors really wanted to help people, they'd discover a way to keep shots from hurting.

DAD: I think they have more important things to work on right now, dear.

VICKI: Jimmy Joe Bryan says people become doctors so they can make other people scream and cry.

DAD: Isn't he the boy who said people become school principals so they can punish children?

VICKI: Yup. He's a really smart guy.

DAD: He's a smart something, that's for sure. The fact remains, you have to get this shot.

VICKI: But it will hurt.

DAD: Only for a moment. And that pain now will save you from great pain later.

VICKI: Why can't it be something that feels good now but still keeps it from being painful later? Like when Grandma says, "Let me kiss it and make it feel better"?

DAD: Because life isn't as easy as we'd like it to be, Vicki. But we can learn from that, too.

VICKI: Is learning always painful?

DAD: Not always, but often, because it involves mistakes and they usually hurt. But if we learn, we can avoid more painful mistakes later.

VICKI: There's no way around this, is there? I have to get this shot.

DAD: See? You're learning.

VICKI: Maybe if I had something wonderful to look forward to afterward, that would help me deal with the pain.

DAD: Something like a double-dip ice cream cone?

VICKI: Hey, Dad, you're learning, too.

(They smile at each other.)

Pure Milk (1 Peter 2:2–3)

Setting: A restaurant table.

NARRATOR: 1 Peter 2:2–3 says, "Like newborn babies, crave pure spiritual milk, so that by it you may grow up in your salvation, now that you have tasted that the Lord is good."

(STEVE, TRISH, and DOUG enter and sit at the table.)

STEVE: This is a great table.

TRISH: Where's the waiter? I am so thirsty. Do you realize how long it's been since I had a drink?

STEVE: Since last night?

TRISH: And that's a long time. I am craving a drink.

STEVE: I could go for one myself.

DOUG: Set me up with a long, cool one.

TRISH: Finally, here's the waiter.

(The WAITER enters and walks up to the table.)

WAITER: Good evening, folks. How is everyone tonight?

TRISH: Dying of thirst.

WAITER: Have we had a busy day?

STEVE: It's been a killer.

WAITER: Well, we'll take wonderful care of you. First, let me tell you about our specials. We have a marvelous blackened red snapper, served with a rice pilaf and our famous Caesar salad. We also have fresh mahi mahi in an artichoke vinaigrette, which comes with steamed vegetables and pan-roasted potatoes. Or, if you're really hungry, there's Beef Wellington, accompanied by redskin potatoes and asparagus in hollandaise sauce.

DOUG: Wow! Those all sound so good.

TRISH: Really, really delicious.

WAITER: We make it hard to decide and we're proud of that.

STEVE: I know what I want.

WAITER: Excellent, sir.

STEVE: I want milk.

TRISH: Make that two.

DOUG: No, make it three.

WAITER: Milk?

TRISH: Pure milk.

WAITER: I see. And for your entree?

TRISH: Oh, no, I'll just have the milk.

STEVE: That'll be fine for me, too.

DOUG: Ditto.

WAITER: Just milk. *(with a deep sigh)* Two percent or skim?

TRISH: Pure.

STEVE: Whole.

DOUG: The really white stuff.

WAITER: Three pure milks. Thank you so much.

(The WAITER rolls his eyes and exits.)

STEVE: The things you have to go through to get a glass of milk these days.

TRISH: Everyone wants to water it down or dress it up.

DOUG: It's always, "Don't you want some chocolate syrup in that?" or "Can I pour it on some pudding for you?"

TRISH: When I was growing up, my family went through two gallons a day. Now, most people put a dash in their coffee, a splash on their cereal, and that's it.

STEVE: That's probably why it's hard to find a good milkman these days — not enough demand. I see soda delivery trucks everywhere I turn, but no milk wagons.

TRISH: People don't think they need the nutrition pure milk provides.

DOUG: And they wonder why they feel dragged down all the time. Calcium deficiency!

(The WAITER enters with a serving tray.)

WAITER: *(as he serves them)* Here are your three pure milks. And I took the liberty of bringing you some of our homemade chocolate chip cookies. After all, what is milk without cookies?

STEVE: Pure!

TRISH: Refreshing!

DOUG: Renewing!

(The WAITER stares in amazement as they push the cookies away and chug down their milk. The WAITER picks up the cookies and exits.)

Do as I Say, Not as I Do (3 John 9–11)

Setting: CHARLIE *sits in a chair, reading the newspaper. There is a telephone table near him.* MOM *enters, racing the clock.*

MOM: Charlie, let's go. You'd better shake a leg or you're going to be late for school.

CHARLIE: I'm almost done, Mom. Just a couple more paragraphs in this excellent story about the Colorado Avalanche.

MOM: There was an avalanche in Colorado? Were many people hurt?

CHARLIE: Mom. The hockey team?

MOM: They were hurt? Let me see that. *(taking the paper from him)* Oh, my goodness.

CHARLIE: Mom, Avalanche is the name of the team.

MOM: Not that. This. *(pointing)* It's the Hudson Twelve-Hour Sale. They only hold it once a year. Prices so low you can't believe them.

CHARLIE: Yeah, so?

MOM: It's today.

CHARLIE: Again I ask — yeah, so?

MOM: It's one of those things you'll understand when you're older, Charlie. A sale like this can't be missed.

*(*MOM *picks up the phone and dials. She speaks in a hoarse whisper.)*

MOM (cont'd): *(into phone)* Hello, Mr. Preston? This is Alice. *(forces a cough)* Yes, Mr. Preston, I've come down with a virus of some kind — cough, cough — maybe even bronchitis — cough, cough — I'm really dragging. The doctor thinks bed rest is the best medicine, so I'm going to stay home today and sleep. I'll try to come in early tomorrow and make up for it. *(pause)* Thank you, Mr. Preston — cough, cough — I'll see you tomorrow. *(hangs up)* All right! Hudson's, here I come! I have some serious shopping to do! *(nudging* CHARLIE*)* Charlie, I told you to shake a leg. Do you want a ride to school or not?

*(*MOM *gathers up her things.* CHARLIE *watches her a moment, then picks up the phone and dials.)*

MOM (cont'd): Charlie, who are you calling?

CHARLIE: The school office.

MOM: Why? You won't be tardy if you go get in the car this minute.

CHARLIE: No, Mom, I need to tell them I won't be in today.

MOM: Excuse me, young man?

CHARLIE: Yeah, I think I'll blow this day off, too. No offense, I'm not going to the Hudson's sale with you, but I would love a ride to the mall.

MOM: Charlie, what on earth makes you think I would let you do such a thing?

CHARLIE: The fact that you just did such a thing.

MOM: That's different.

CHARLIE: Oh, man, like I didn't see that one coming. Grown-ups always use that one when you don't have a good reason to give us. *(mimicking)* "That's different."

MOM: The fact of the matter is, it is different.

CHARLIE: How?

MOM: Well...for one thing, I've already finished high school. *(responding to Charlie's look)* Okay, and for another thing, this is a once-a-year sale.

CHARLIE: I still say you're copping out.

MOM: This is not open for discussion, Charlie. Do as I say, not as I do.

CHARLIE: Man, another classic hit. "Do as I say, not as I do."

MOM: This is one of those things you'll understand when you're older.

CHARLIE: What's to understand? You wanna go blow some money at the mall on things you don't really need, so you lied to your boss and bailed out on him.

MOM: That's really oversimplifying it, Charlie. As an adult, I have a lot of pressure and stress —

CHARLIE: You think trigonometry is a beach party or something?

MOM: *(pause, then)* You're absolutely right. You got me.

CHARLIE: All right! Mental health day for two!

MOM: Oh, no, you're not skipping school.

CHARLIE: But you just said —

MOM: I'm going to work. I call myself a Christian, and yet I am willing to lie. And over something so meaningless. And, worst of all, in front of you. I should be an example to you, and instead I tell you not to follow my example, to do as I say and not as I do. I'm ashamed of myself. Mr. Preston is going to be very surprised to see me, but you've made me wake up to my error.

CHARLIE: Come on, Mom, I didn't mean to make a federal case out of it. I can tell you feel bad. Why don't we sit down and talk this out, maybe even pray about it?

MOM: Tonight, Charlie.

CHARLIE: But I think *now* is the time, while it's fresh in your mind — just a couple of hours —

MOM: Charlie!

CHARLIE: I know, I know. "Shake a leg!"

Prayer-Paration

Setting: KEN *and* TOM *are sitting on a bench, watching a swim meet.*

KEN: Come on, Philip! You can do it, son!

(KEN *claps in encouragement, then folds his hands in prayer, and bows his head.)*

KEN (cont'd): Lord, please help Philip win this race. Lift him up out of the waters and carry him to the finish line first, ahead of all the other contestants. Lord, you know we've been in church every Sunday for the last month. We ask that you reward our attendance with a gold medal in this 200-yard freestyle contest. Amen.

TOM: What are you doing?

KEN: Just saying a little prayer for my boy. He's in lane seven. *(calling)* Go, Philip!

TOM: My boy's in lane four.

KEN: Oh. Sorry he's not going to win.

TOM: What makes you so sure? And why should God help your son win instead of any of the other seven kids down there, including mine?

KEN: Well, I... We have been going to church quite a lot lately.

TOM: Let's thump our Bibles and sing Hallelujah! Do you really think you can say a little prayer and your son will win?

KEN: "Ask and it shall be given."

TOM: So suppose I ask God for my son to win.

KEN: Too late. I prayed before you did. It's kind of a "first dibs" thing, far as I can tell.

TOM: Are you trying to tell me that my son's 5:30 a.m. workouts, after-school practices, off-season weight training, and strict diet have nothing to do with the outcome of this race? Are you telling me that God doesn't care about all the time and effort my son has put in to developing the talents God gave him? That it all boils down to one pre-race prayer?

KEN: I've obviously offended you. How 'bout I make it up to you by praying for a tie? *(starting to pray)* Hey, Lord, me again. I—

TOM: No way. I am not letting you off the hook that easily. Where did you get the idea that you can substitute prayer for hard work and discipline? Do you really think that's what God wants for us?

KEN: I don't claim to be a Bible scholar.

TOM: But you are a prayer expert? A little bended knee and your son is an Olympic champion. Next thing you know, he'll be endorsing swim goggles and breakfast cereal. All because his dad can pray to win.

KEN: This is amazing. I read in the Bible that God's people are persecuted because of their faith, but I never expected it to happen to me.

TOM: You think I'm persecuting you?

KEN: What would you call it? Bullying?

TOM: I'm trying to talk some sense into you.

KEN: You're trying to ruin my relationship with God.

TOM: What kind of relationship can you have with him when you treat him like Santa Claus instead of your Lord and Savior?

KEN: Perhaps if you attended church regularly, you'd see things differently.

TOM: Buddy, I see your kind all the time. Think God exists to grant their every wish. That God created the world to revolve around them. It's enough to make me want to stay home and not go to church at all some weeks.

KEN: There's your mistake. You need to go to church every Sunday. And this Sunday, I encourage you to pray about this and remember: "Ask and it shall be given unto you."

TOM: Maybe the pastor should try your system instead of preparing this week's sermon. "Lord, I didn't take the time to prepare a message this week. I went to swim meets and watched TV instead. So, when I get in the pulpit, make it happen for me, Lord." *(getting up to leave)* It could revolutionize church as we know it. Think of all the hours of work the pastor would save. And I should know. I'm a pastor!

(TOM exits.)

Fold, Stuff, and Seal

Setting: ELMO *sits at the table, stuffing envelopes.* MR. WILSON *enters with* BETTY.

MR. WILSON: Here we are, Betty. This is where you'll be working. And this is your colleague, Elmo. He stuffs five hundred of these things each day.

ELMO: *(continuing to work)* Hi!

BETTY: Hello.

MR. WILSON: Have a seat, Betty. *(as she does)* Now as I told you, this is your typical "fold, stuff, and seal" job. Fold the letter, stuff it in the envelope, and seal it shut — just as Elmo is doing.

BETTY: No problem, Mr. Wilson. I think I've got it.

MR. WILSON: Fine. You get a ten-minute break at ten-o'clock, thirty minutes for lunch, and another ten minute break at two-thirty. Any questions?

BETTY: No, sir, I'm all set.

MR. WILSON: Best of luck to you.

(MR. WILSON *exits.* BETTY *begins working.* ELMO *continues to work for a moment, then looks to be sure* MR. WILSON *has gone.* ELMO *stops working and sits back. He watches* BETTY *for a few moments.)*

ELMO: Take a break, Betty.

BETTY: *(not stopping)* But I just started. And it's not ten o'clock yet.

ELMO: I know, but he's gone.

BETTY: Who's gone?

ELMO: Ol' Man Wilson, the taskmaster. He's gone.

BETTY: Yes, I know that. What difference does that make?

ELMO: It means you can kick back and relax.

BETTY: *(stopping)* You mean, goof off?

ELMO: That's such an ugly term. I prefer to think of it as "pacing myself." Ol' Man Wilson thinks I can do five hundred of these things a day. I got news for you and him — I could do twice that if I wanted to.

BETTY: *(starting again)* Why don't you?

ELMO: Are you kidding? Bust a gut for this lousy job?

BETTY: But you're being paid to work eight hours.

ELMO: And I make the work fill eight hours. Pacing, Betty, it's all about pacing. I've got a deck of cards. Wanna play gin rummy?

BETTY: No!

ELMO: Not a game-player, huh? That's fine. I brought the paper, too.

(He takes out the newspaper and begins reading. BETTY continues stuffing at a good pace. After a few moments, ELMO looks over his paper at her.)

ELMO (cont'd): Hey, you're going pretty fast over there.

BETTY: Just doing my job.

ELMO: Keep it up and you could break a thousand today.

BETTY: Could be.

ELMO: So, knock it off!

BETTY: I beg your pardon.

ELMO: If you do a thousand and I only do five hundred, how's that going to make me look?

BETTY: Like you were "pacing yourself."

ELMO: No, like I was goofing off. And Ol' Man Wilson doesn't like goof-offs. You're going to get me fired!

BETTY: Look, Elmo, what you do with your time is your business. But I was hired to do this job, not play cards or read the newspaper. And I don't feel right about being paid if I don't think I earned it. It goes against my convictions and beliefs.

ELMO: Oh, great. A religious fanatic, too.

BETTY: I'm a Christian. If that makes me a fanatic in your book, so be it. But my beliefs teach me to be honest with everyone, including my employer.

ELMO: Isn't this peachy. I get to work with a saint who takes her work seriously. What is the world coming to?

BETTY: I'm sorry if it disturbs you, Elmo, but it really is the right thing to do.

ELMO: *(starting to work again)* God help me.

BETTY: He will, Elmo. He will give you plenty to fill your heart, but you have to do the folding, stuffing, and sealing on your own.

NARRATOR: The Apostle Paul wrote, "Whatever you do [in your work], work at it with all your heart, as working for the Lord."

The Church of the Crutch

Setting: A church narthex. SANDY and BEN enter, SANDY on crutches and BEN with a cane.

SANDY: The nerve of that pastor.

BEN: I'm stunned that he would dare suggest such a thing.

SANDY: I think pastors just lose touch with the real world sometimes.

BEN: Must be all that time they spend studying the Bible and praying. Makes them too idealistic.

SANDY: Ours is living in a dream world, that's for sure.

(JUNE enters, also on crutches.)

JUNE: Hi, guys.

SANDY: Hi, June.

JUNE: Can you believe that pastor of ours? Where does he get these crazy ideas?

BEN: We were just talking about that.

JUNE: I don't know about you two, but there's no way I'm going to invite a friend to come to this church until we get the nursery remodeled.

SANDY: That project seems to be limping along.

JUNE: The nursery is still an eyesore. If the pastor expects me to invite my friends to come and see that room in its sorry state, he's dreaming. Once it's finished and refurnished, then I'll be able to invite friends.

BEN: I don't mind the nursery so much. It's the choir that's crippling us. I've thought several times about inviting my neighbor to worship. But she's a piano teacher and a member of the Community Chorus, and I am not going to invite her to come and listen to our teeny-tiny choir and wheezy old organ. If we had a stronger music program, I'd bring her next week, but the way things are now — forget it.

SANDY: You both have valid concerns, but what's really crippling this church is the lack of young single men and women. I mean, I have tons of young single friends at work who are looking for a good church home, but how can I invite them here when we have nothing but families? I can't invite them until we have an effective singles ministry in place.

(RICK enters, also on crutches.)

RICK: Can you folks believe what Pastor wants us to do? Bring friends to church? How can I do that when there aren't any teams for them to join once they've worshiped with us? I'm embarrassed that we don't have a softball or basketball team. Heck, I'd invite someone if we had a simple lousy bowling team, but we don't even have that.

JUNE: How can Pastor ask us to bring people here when there's so much wrong with the church? Does he wants us to feel ashamed?

(BOB walks by with a friend. Neither is on crutches.)

BOB: Hi, everyone! See you next Sunday!

(BOB and his friend exit.)

SANDY: That Bob is always so upbeat.

BEN: He's as out of touch as the pastor. He's always bringing a friend to church, so he obviously doesn't see the problems that we see.

RICK: Another dreamer.

JUNE: No shame.

SANDY: See you all next week.

(They all start to exit, but their canes and crutches get tangled for a moment, and they almost knock each other down. They carefully separate themselves and back away from each other.)

BEN: One more problem we have to fix!

(They all nod and grumble and go their separate ways.)

Aunts and Uncles

Setting: BILL *sits reading a magazine as* MOM *enters.*

MOM: Bill, I want you to know that we are celebrating Thanksgiving as a family at Uncle Herman's this year. I'm telling you now so you don't schedule anything else. Much as I know you would like to.

BILL: Mom, don't torture me like this. Do I have to go?

MOM: Do I really need to answer?

BILL: But it's the same deal every year. Aunt Gertrude will pinch my cheeks and tell me I'm "a fine-looking young pup." And Uncle Jack will sit down, stare at me about ten minutes, and then ask me what he asks me every year: "How old are you now, Bill?" And this just might be the year that I tell him, "One year older than the last time you asked me."

MOM: William James, don't you dare.

BILL: Mom, the guy's like eight hundred, and sure, he can quote Stan Musial's batting average for every major league season, but he can't remember how old I am?

MOM: Uncle Jack is just trying to make conversation with you.

BILL: He doesn't need to go out of his way on my account. Or Uncle Sylvester, either. If I have to hear about being in a foxhole behind enemy lines in fifteen-degree weather one more time — I'll put a grenade in his mashed potatoes.

MOM: Bill, this is your family that you're talking about. How about showing a little love and compassion?

BILL: It would be easier if they were a little more interesting, Mom. But they're all hung up on the past and how great it was. It's like Uncle Willy's wardrobe — didn't anybody tell the guy that disco is dead?

MOM: Bill, I know you're always thinking about the future and anxious to get on with your life, but you need to develop an appreciation for where your relatives have been and what they've done in their lives.

BILL: Mom, the world is changing too fast for me to even think about the past.

MOM: Maybe that's why Uncle Sylvester keeps telling his foxhole story and Aunt Betsy talks about the one-room schoolhouse and maybe even why Uncle Willy still wears his leisure suits. The past is all they have that doesn't change.

BILL: And they're welcome to it. As for me, they can keep radio and black-and-white TV. I am a child of the Internet.

MOM: Oh, this is so familiar. I used to complain about my aunts and uncles the same way.

BILL: And did your mom and dad let you off the hook?

MOM: No, they explained to me the importance of our family's history. And I realized how lucky I was to hear it from the people who had lived it. Trust me, Bill, as the years go by, these stories will become more and more dear to you, each one a piece in our family quilt.

BILL: Oh, that'll be the day, Mom. I'll hold my breath until that one rolls around.

MOM: Bill, one day, these stories will be all you'll have to connect you to people who are gone.

BILL: Wow! I hadn't thought about them... being gone. All that will be left is the stories. And I'll have to tell them to the next generation. Like the Jewish people today, when they tell the Exodus story every year at Passover.

MOM: So you do stay awake in Sunday school. I'm so pleased.

BILL: But appreciating the past doesn't mean I have to live in the past, Mom.

MOM: That's true. The past should help you prepare for the future, not be your future. Which is something we should mention to Uncle Willy in regard to his wardrobe.

BILL: This has really gotten me thinking, Mom. And it raises one very serious, pretty frightening question.

MOM: What's that?

BILL: One day, will my nieces and nephews complain to their parents about having to listen to me?

MOM: Bingo!

BILL: Oh, man. Then I have a lot of work to do.

(He starts out.)

MOM: Bill, where are you going?

BILL: I'm going out to have such wild adventures that my nieces and nephews will want to hear about them.

(He exits. MOM shakes her head, laughing.)

MOM: What a kidder. *(reconsidering)* Wait a minute. *(calling)* Bill?

(She hurries after him.)

Bumper Stickers and Cross Necklaces

Setting: An office hallway. PAM *and* BETH *walk together.*

PAM: I can't understand it. Jim still hasn't accepted Christ.

BETH: Why does that surprise you?

PAM: Because I've done just about everything humanly possible.

BETH: Such as?

PAM: Every chance I get, I slip a spiritual tract into his coat pocket. Last week, I left him a great one. On the cover it says in these drippy, blood-red letters, "IF YOU DON'T HAVE JESUS, GOD'S GOING TO SQUASH YOU LIKE A BUG."

BETH: And that didn't sway him.

PAM: Two days later, I invited him to go to church with me. I figured I had planted the seed with the tract, so he'd be open to the invitation. I was even wearing my "Jesus is the solid rock" T-shirt, the cute one with all the sequins. But he said he was going to be busy.

BETH: And that's all you've done?

PAM: Holy cow, no. I invited him to an evangelistic revival service, but he said he was going to the movies. He invited me to go with him.

BETH: Great! And...

PAM: I saw this as my big chance, the open door, the Spirit-directed opportunity to bring him into the Kingdom.

BETH: Wonderful. What movie did you see?

PAM: I didn't go with him, silly. I instructed him in how Hollywood is the new Sodom and Gomorrah and that's why they have all those earthquakes out there, because God is preparing to wipe them off the face of the earth and He just might take all the movie theaters at the same time, so we should all steer clear. And I told him I was telling him all this in the spirit of loving witness to the Lord.

BETH: So that was it. No movie.

PAM: No, and he just stared at me like I was an idiot. He doesn't get it. And I don't know how to help him to the truth, because now he won't even talk to me.

BETH: Because of the movie speech?

PAM: No, because I put a bumper sticker on his car without asking.

BETH: He drives a really nice car.

PAM: Well, it's a really nice bumper sticker. It said, "THE DRIVER OF THIS CAR IS GOING TO HELL."

BETH: In drippy, blood-red letters?

PAM: Of course. Obviously, it forced him to confront the possibility of eternal damnation, and he didn't like what he saw.

BETH: Maybe you need a new approach.

PAM: What's left? I've tried lapel pins, huge cross necklaces, my gospel socks with "John 3:16" printed all over them. I've even sent him cards that say, "Thinking of you. Repent or go to hell!" But I'm not any closer to saving him than when I first started.

BETH: Have you tried radical love?

PAM: Radical love? Sounds pretty leftist and liberal to me.

BETH: Not at all. It's what Jesus practiced and preached. You know, going the extra mile.

PAM: I get it! I'll put tracts in both his pockets!

BETH: No, I mean loving Jim for who he is. Stop talking about hell and start showing him heaven through the love of Jesus.

PAM: So you would definitely nix the "Battle of Armageddon" balloon bouquet.

BETH: Absolutely.

PAM: I don't know. All love, no fear. Sounds pretty unorthodox.

BETH: You think the cross was run-of-the-mill?

PAM: No, it was pretty radical. And the result — completely radical. *(pause)* Maybe I'll go see if Jim would like to split a pizza.

BETH: Just don't order onions on it.

PAM: Why? What's the spiritual significance of onions?

BETH: I have no idea. I just know they give you heartburn.

(They exit.)

Sensible Worship

Setting: Rows of chairs to suggest pews. ANDY *and* GIL *sit in the front row. As they converse, their conversation is expressionless and monotone.*

ANDY: Morning.

GIL: Morning.

ANDY: Good to see you at worship this morning.

GIL: Glad to see you, too.

ANDY: Always the highlight of my week.

GIL: Couldn't get along without it.

ANDY: A stimulating spiritual exercise.

GIL: A mountain-top experience.

*(*ANDY *and* GIL *settle into their chairs and start to nod off.* ERIC *enters and sits behind them. He is smiling, wide awake, and full of energy. He looks straight ahead, past* ANDY *and* GIL*, who are now asleep. After a moment,* ERIC *stands.)*

ERIC: Hallelujah!

*(*ANDY *and* GIL *jump, startled out of sleep. They look back at* ERIC*, who is oblivious to their stares. He sits down, and they turn back around and slowly nod off again. After a few moments,* ERIC *jumps up again.)*

ERIC: Praise the Lord!

*(*ANDY *and* GIL *jump again.)*

ANDY: Excuse me.

ERIC: Yes?

ANDY: Are you visiting with us today?

ERIC: Yes, I am. And I just praise the Lord that I have been blessed in finding a nice, friendly church to worship in.

GIL: Are you always this...vocal when you worship?

ERIC: Is Jesus our Lord? The answer to both questions is, of course!

ANDY: That's very nice, but we're used to a quieter, more contemplative worship experience and you're making it very difficult for us to concentrate, jumping up and making all that noise.

ERIC: I had no idea. I'll try to be quieter.

GIL: It's all right, you're new. Mistakes are to be expected.

(ERIC sits down. ANDY and GIL nod off again. ERIC struggles and squirms for a moment, then leaps back up.)

ERIC: Jesus is Lord! Hallelujah! Praise his name!

(ANDY and GIL jump, and this time they stand to face Eric.)

GIL: What did we tell you?

ERIC: I'm sorry, I'm sorry. I tried to hold it in, but my joy in the Lord is too great to contain. I just have to make a joyful noise!

ANDY: Come on, Gil. Let's sit over in front of the pulpit. We can worship in peace over there.

GIL: Right behind you, Andy. Some people are so insensitive. No respect for others. How are we supposed to get anything out of the service when he's making such a racket?

(They walk away. ERIC tries to contain himself again, then throws his arms up in the air.)

ERIC: Hallelujah!